Reflections of an Abundant Heart

Lessons From Nature and Life

Wanda Strange

Dedication

To the glory of my Lord and Savior, Jesus Christ

*May these words of my mouth and this
meditation of my heart be pleasing in your
sight, LORD, my Rock and my Redeemer.
(Psalm 19:14 NIV).*

Contents

Acknowledgments i

An Awesome Reason to Search the Skies.......................... 1

Do I Have Your Full Attention?...................................... 5

Finding the Way through the Fog 8

Be Still and Know.. 11

Bluebonnets in the Snow 16

Gloomy Skies 20

All Wet.. 23

Sonshine Reflected 28

Inner Strength 31

Hot and Dry... 34

Devastating Storms.. 37

Stand Firm.. 40

Raging Waters 43

The Eye of God 46

Restoration by Still Waters... 50

Stay Alert.. 54

Night Lights 57

Royal Colors of Morning 61

Total Eclipse 64

Full Moon 67

History and Symbols of Advent...................................... 71

Keep the Flame Burning.. 76

Peace Beyond Human Understanding............................. 80

Firm Foundation; Then What... 85

Restoring Joy.. 91

Tell the Old Stories 96

Replenishing Hope 102

A View from the Top 106

Wishing on a Star.. 110

Lost in the Moment... 114

No Problem * Don't Worry * Be Happy...................... 117

Pruning for Beauty and Fruitfulness........................... 120

Quench the Thirst 124

The Voice of Experience 127

Altered Perception.. 131

The Colors of Spring 134

Grazing in Unexpected Places..................................... 138

Living Waters 142

Scattered Light.. 146

You Cast, He'll Catch 149

Living with Threatening Skies 153

Miracle on the Highway.. 157

The Pathway to Royalty 161

Eagles Are Not the Only Birds That Soar 164

The Real Thing... 168

Changing Skies.. 171

Requirements.. 175

A Higher Way... 178

Flight of the Butterfly 182

Amazing Love 186

Glimpses of Holiness, ... 191

A Christmas Reflection 191

He is Coming Back... 195

References 198

About the Author... 199

Acknowledgments

I gratefully acknowledge:

my family whose encouragement enables me to explore my creative side and keep me grounded

the army of faithful prayer warriors upon whom I can depend

to my friends who shared insights sparking some reflections

Living Waters writing critique group who hold each other accountable and offer constructive criticism

To my sister, Lisa Bell, for her expertise and constant encouragement.

To the reader
I pray God will use my words to spark gratitude in
your heart.
As the scripture, my reflections, or prayers resonate
with you,
record your personal response, prayers, and praises.
As Holy Spirit speaks to your heart, write the
messages God gives you.
I pray His rich blessings on your life
as you seek Him with your whole heart.

Wanda Strange

"For I know the plans I have for you," declares the LORD, "plans to prosper you and not to harm you, plans to give you hope and a future. Then you will call on me and come and pray to me, and I will listen to you. You will seek me and find me when you seek me with all your heart."
(Jeremiah 29: 11-13 NIV)

An Awesome Reason to Search the Skies

God's Word

When they were together for the last time they asked, "Master, are you going to restore the kingdom to Israel now? Is this the time?"

He told them, "You don't get to know the time. Timing is the Father's business. What you'll get is the Holy Spirit. And when the Holy Spirit comes on you, you will be able to be my witnesses in Jerusalem, all over Judea and Samaria, even to the ends of the world."

These were his last words. As they watched, he was taken up and disappeared in a cloud. They stood there, staring into the empty sky. Suddenly two men appeared—in white robes! They said, "You Galileans! Why do you just stand here looking up at an empty sky? This very Jesus who was taken up from among you to heaven will come as certainly—and mysteriously—as he left." (Acts 1: 6-11 The Message).

Reflection of an Abundant Heart

For more than four decades, I commuted to one medical office or another. For almost thirty years we lived in a DFW suburb before moving to our current country home.

Never obsessed with luxury vehicles, I required only affordable, reliable transportation. Heat, air, and a radio with CD player (sadly, no longer available in new models) fulfilled my accessory demands.

I shudder to think how many actual miles I logged, or how many hours I spent on the road. Time spent in the car varied from one to four hours each work day. During my professional career, I literally wore out five cars.

One morning God used an "Aha Moment" to speak to my spirit and change my attitude about commute time. Instead of stressing over traffic, I determined to search the horizon and look for God to reveal Himself through nature and events.

God set in motion a world designed to evoke amazement and inspire worship. The smallest details can open our eyes to the wonder around us.

When Jesus ascended to heaven, his disciples stood gazing into the sky. They must have wondered what just happened. How long did they stand there before the angels appeared?

Imagine the conversation.

"Where did He go?"

"Wait a minute! What did He say? "

"We get the Holy Spirit? What exactly does that mean? What does it look like?"

"We are to be witnesses? Of what? Where? When?"

Their grief magnified the confusion swirling in their heads. Astonished, they stood, not sure what to do next.

The sky held no answers for the disciples and may not hold solutions for our hearts today.

However, the skies do contain wonders and lead us to reflect on truths found in God's word.

On a given day, I may receive a profound revelation. On another, the presence of Holy Spirit may offer the comfort I need for a moment in time.

As I journey through life, whether commuting, traveling for pleasure, or simply taking a walk, I search the skies.

With an open heart, I earnestly seek Him.

One day, Jesus will reappear as suddenly as he left. When He returns, I hope He finds me faithfully searching the skies.

Prayer of an Abundant Heart

Dear Precious Jesus,
I earnestly seek you and desire to abide in the presence of Holy Spirit.
I open my heart to you and ask you to reveal the truth you have for me
today.
As I travel through life, I ask you to show me the wonders you want
me to see.
I pray you will open my eyes to the needs of those around me.
Make me always aware of the skies.
You might come any day. I want to be looking up when you return.

Reflection of an Abundant Heart

_____

_____

_____

_____

_____

_____

_____

_____

_____

_____

_____

_____

_____

_____

_____

Do I Have Your Full Attention?

God's Word

Meanwhile, Saul was still breathing out murderous threats against the Lord's disciples. He went to the high priest and asked him for letters to the synagogues in Damascus, so that if he found any there who belonged to the Way, whether men or women, he might take them as prisoners to Jerusalem. As he neared Damascus on his journey, suddenly a light from heaven flashed around him. He fell to the ground and heard a voice say to him, "Saul, Saul, why do you persecute me?"

"Who are you, Lord?" Saul asked.

"I am Jesus, whom you are persecuting," he replied.

"Now get up and go into the city, and you will be told what you must do." (Acts 9: 1-6 NIV).

Reflection of an Abundant Heart

The early morning drive to the east can be brutal. I reach for my sunglasses. I sit up taller and adjust the visor in an attempt to block the blinding sun. I even pick up a magazine from the passenger seat and hold it strategically to shield my eyes. I allow safe distance from the cars in the lane ahead.

The light interrupts my racing thoughts. Temporarily, I set aside plans for the busy day ahead. I focus only on blocking the light and the road ahead which demands my full attention. Otherwise, I will find myself in a ditch, or worse colliding with another vehicle.

Is this the kind of light God used to capture Saul's attention?

Most days, my life moves at a breakneck pace—running from place to place—appointment to appointment—meeting to meeting.

Do I take a single moment to acknowledge God's presence, provision, and protection?

I justify my actions.

People depend on me. Nothing on my agenda is bad or harmful, is it?

Certainly, I'm not out to persecute Christians, like Saul was.

I'll get around to prayer and time in God's Word later today.

Then life intrudes, and my time with the Lord gets put on the back burner. Soon I'm running on empty as I attempt to serve Him in my own strength.

The brilliant light persists. Rather than diverting my eyes, I refocus my spiritual eyes on Jesus, determined to reorder my priorities and give Him my full attention.

Prayer of an Abundant Heart
Lord Jesus,
Forgive me when I rush ahead of you, so busy trying to serve you
without first seeking your presence and your guidance.
I acknowledge my need of your power in every aspect of my life.
Thank You for never giving up on me, relentlessly pursuing me —
using whatever means to remind me to turn to you.
I gratefully acknowledge your faithfulness.
Help me to walk in the sunlight of your love.

Personal Reflection

_____

_____

_____

_____

_____

_____

_____

_____

_____

_____

_____

_____

_____

_____

_____

_____

_____

_____

_____

_____

_____

_____

_____

_____

_____

_____

_____

_____

Finding the Way through the Fog

God's Word
Thy word is a lamp unto my feet and a light unto my path. *(Psalm 119:105 KJV)*

Reflection of an Abundant Heart
Five o'clock in the morning, the densest fog I ever encountered obscures everything beyond a few feet. Pulling out of the driveway, the only light available comes from the headlights of my own vehicle. The soupy atmosphere completely negates any light the moon and stars, usually bright this time of the morning, typically provides. Nothing in my experience prepares me for this darkness.

This morning certainly tests my driving skills as I can see only a few feet in front of me. Driving through the country in this type of weather presents special challenges. The other vehicles can't see me any better than I can see them. Animals, darting across the road, fail to conceive the added danger the soupy condition presents to them or the drivers they might encounter.

A wiser person would return home and wait for a little more sunlight or for the low-lying clouds to lift. However, being devoted to my goal and feeling somewhat bullet proof, I continue to travel the highway to the city. Much to my relief, a car appears before me. I adjust my speed and remain a safe distance behind the vehicle in the lane ahead, employing its tail lights to guide me safely down the road. I simply need to keep the leader in my sights. Knowing the route, I will recognize if the lead car takes a different direction than the one leading to my destination. Being less familiar with the road or following blindly, I might easily be led astray.

Frequently, my spiritual journey resembles driving in the dark through a dense mist. More often than I care to admit, I find myself in a haze.

What is my next step?

Which direction should I take?

How fast should I move?

Perhaps I should be still for a little while and wait for clarity.

As we walk in faith together, Christian friends may illuminate God's Word. Sometimes they offer honest communication and other times by actions. Mentors, people of faith with conviction and commitment, encourage growth and share truth in love. At times, it may be appropriate to follow, being led by the light of someone else's experience. Other times, we appropriately step out, take the lead and blaze a trail.

Valuable lessons from this experience provide fresh perspective. Navigating challenges in uncertain situations requires knowledge of the route, carefully choosing who and how to follow. Listen for direction from Holy Spirit, and measure every decision by the standard of God's Word.

Prayer of an Abundant Heart

Guide me, Jehovah God.

Hold me accountable for those who follow my leadership.

Give me wisdom as I choose Godly mentors.

Help me to trust you when the way is unclear.

Give me enough light to take the next step.

Personal Reflection

_____

_____

_____

_____

_____

_____

_____

_____

_____

_____

_____

_____

_____

_____

_____

_____

_____

_____

_____

_____

_____

_____

_____

_____

_____

Be Still and Know

God's Word

Be still and know that I am God: I will be exalted among the nations; I will be exalted in the earth. (Psalm 46:10 NIV).

Reflection of an Abundant Heart

The original downtown Dallas El Fenix stands as a favorite Wednesday night destination for many area Dallasites. In the early seventies, the Wednesday night, enchilada dinner special cost $0.99. Today the same special, priced significantly more, remains the best bargain in town. One April afternoon. several of my co-workers and I met for dinner, something we did frequently. As I pulled into the parking lot, menacing clouds predicted a coming storm. Not overly concerned, I proceeded into the restaurant.

The storm will pass, and traffic will clear out while we're eating. I'm off for the next two days. I can use the two-hour drive home to decompress.

As I exited the car, my cell phone rang. My husband updated me on weather conditions reported on the local news cast. Concerned about me driving through the storm, he cautioned me to stay in a safe place. My co-workers and I enjoyed a leisurely dinner, while we waited out the storm. When we exited the building, the sky cleared. No ominous signs remained.

I drove through a familiar area of downtown, though it had been some time since my commute had taken me that direction. A prominent highway sign—I-35 South.

Great! A new entrance will lead to a shorter route to where I need to go!

Little did I realize I entered the HOV lane, High Occupancy Vehicle. Though not exactly sure what qualified as high occupancy, I knew one person definitely did not. I might have been ticketed, but soon the violation of a traffic regulation became least of my concerns. Torrential rain fell the minute I entered the ramp into a lane lined with concrete barricades. Even on dry, clear days, I hated those barriers. Though I never considered myself to be claustrophobic, those concrete walls felt as if the road closed in on me. In addition to sheets of rain, strong wind gusts demanded every ounce of my strength and concentration to keep the car steady. I looked for an exit, to pull off the highway and wait for the pouring rain to stop. However, I saw no way off and nowhere to go. Though not in my line of vision, I sensed other vehicles occupied the lanes beside me, and I feared being hit by an unseen car.

Eventually, the lane ended, and I safely exited the freeway. I headed to a nearby Starbucks, called my husband, calmed down, and waited out the storm. I later learned the area of Oak Cliff I traveled had been the hardest hit that night. Definitely shaken and grateful for a secure building, I took time to regain stability. I learned valuable lessons that evening.

Listen to the forecast and heed the warning signs. If I had been aware of the coming storm and waited another half hour, I could have avoided the trauma. Many of life's storms come without warning… the car accident, an illness, or perhaps financial reversals. Other times, warning signs alert us to the trouble ahead. Whether the crisis is unexpected or predicted, close communion with God is the only way to prepare for the wreckage with which we may have to deal. Spiritual discipline allows us to recognize the warning signs and pay attention to God's leadership. Do I go or stay? Which direction? Now or later?

Know the territory. If I had taken a familiar road, I might have had a difficult time, but at least I would have known the way home. The familiar route would offer a safe destination to wait out danger. Taking a new and different route, put me in unexplored areas and made the journey more difficult. The time to explore a new direction is definitely not in the middle of a crisis.

The Bible serves as our roadmap with examples of those who weathered tempests well and others who suffered dire consequences. Being part of the community of faith, gives us fellow travelers to share their experiences as storm chasers and survivors.

Most importantly the experience taught me to stop and be still. Once stopped, I allowed the storm to pass. As long as I continued to struggle, each mile grew more perilous than the last. Persisting in doing things my own way only put me in greater danger. The dark of the storm presented pitfalls I could not foresee.

Most parents understand what it is like to watch a child struggle with a task. Defiantly, a young child may express the desire, "I'll do it myself."

Sometimes, the task needs to be mastered, and the parent allows the child to work out a solution. However, no loving, caring parent allows their child to be in harm's way without comfort. When necessary, the parent steps in to rescue the child they love.

How would you respond if your child cried out to you "help me!"

Wouldn't you do all in your power to meet the need?

I envision God, my Heavenly Father, watching me struggle, waiting for me to simply stop. He waits, patiently for me to be still, acknowledge Him, and ask Him to take over the wreckage left by the tornados of my life.

Prayer of an Abundant Heart
Abba Father, My Papa, My Daddy,
Thank you for keeping me safe, for all the times you rescue me,
and for the peace and calm you provide in the midst of the crisis. Forgive
me when I fail to recognize your authority.
Though the storms of life may continue to rage, you have the power to
calm me, your anxious child and sustain me through difficult
circumstances.

Personal Reflection

_____
_____
_____
_____
_____
_____
_____
_____
_____
_____
_____
_____
_____
_____
_____
_____

_____

_____

_____

_____

_____

_____

_____

_____

_____

_____

_____

_____

_____

_____

_____

_____

_____

_____

_____

_____

_____

_____

_____

_____

_____

Bluebonnets in the Snow

God's Word

For God so loved the world that He gave His only begotten son, that whosoever believeth in Him, should not perish but have everlasting life. (John 3: 16 KJV).

Reflection of an Abundant Heart

According to Texas Legend, long ago a young Comanche girl, She-Who-Is-Alone, listened as the Shaman and tribal leaders discussed the reason for the famine and draught. Her parents and grandparents died, leaving her alone with only one thing to treasure. Her warrior doll wore beaded leggings and a headdress with brilliant-colored feathers from a blue jay. The young girl waited until everyone slept, then slipped away, built a fire. and offered her doll as a sacrifice to the Great Spirits.

When the flames died down, she scooped up the ashes and flung them to the four winds. Her cheeks wet with tears; she lay down and fell asleep. The next morning, she awoke to find the fields covered in beautiful blue flowers as brilliant as the feathers of her beloved doll's headdress. According to the legend, every spring the Great Spirit remembers the sacrifice of the young girl and covers the hills and valleys of Texas with beautiful blue flowers.

Named for its color and resemblance of the petals of a woman's sunbonnet, the bluebonnet blooms each year in early spring, creating a breathtaking display of color and providing a source of pride for Texans. In 1901, Texas adopted the bluebonnet as its state flower.

Readily found in fields and along the roadsides throughout central and south Texas, bluebonnets provide the perfect backdrop for photographers. On any given spring afternoon, professional and amateurs try to capture the perfect image of the bluebonnets, or more correctly, the image of someone special surrounded by a field of bluebonnets. Brides, children in their Easter finery, or babies on blankets surrounded by a solid sheet of blue flowers provide subjects for the camera lens. Several years ago, early spring rains and unseasonably warm temperatures yielded a magnificent show of Texas wildflowers, beginning with the appearance of the bluebonnets. All along the interstate brilliant blue flowers blanketed the medians and roadsides. Since draught and late freezes marred the previous year's production of wildflowers, nature lovers especially appreciated the spectacular display. The week prior to Easter, meteorologists forecasted colder temperatures.

Sure, the optimists thought, it always gets a little colder for Easter, but the spring clothes will still make an appearance, maybe with a little jacket added to the ensemble.

On Saturday before Easter, it snowed. Most observers assumed, no way this will stick. The ground is too warm.

But it stuck, clinging to the trees, blanketing the ground and hills. A beautiful layer of white covering the ground with clean innocence. It appeared more like Christmas than Easter. A most amazing sight – one even the most seasoned Texans never experienced. Bluebonnets peaked through the snow.

Christmas and Easter linked in an amazingly beautiful reminder. Without Christmas, there can be no Easter, and without Easter, Christmas is meaningless.

Prayer of an Abundant Heart

Christ of Christmas and of Easter,
Thank you for the yearly display of beautiful wildflowers, reminding me
of your faithfulness.
As I celebrate the joy of Christmas and Easter, make me mindfully
grateful of your sacrifice, the assurance of eternal life,
and the hope Your resurrection promises.
I thankfully praise you for this wonderful gift.
Empower me with boldness to share the good news with those I meet.

Personal Reflection

Gloomy Skies

God's Word

Take my yoke upon you and learn from me, for I am gentle and humble in heart, and you will find rest for your souls. For my yoke is easy and my burden is light. (Matthew 11:29-30 NIV).

Reflection of an Abundant Heart

Gloomy skies without a ray of sunshine. A thick haze creates an overcast and menacing atmosphere. The sun seems incapable of breaking through dense cloud cover. The heavy atmosphere matches an unidentified sadness, a despair in my heart.

The news details one tragedy after another. I grieve personal losses. The immediate crisis over, I resume the busyness of living day to day. My body and my spirit ache with exhaustion.

Before leaving the house, I apply makeup, masking my tender heart.

I must leave my personal struggles at the door, when I step into my professional caregiver role. Put on a smile and reach out to lift another's burden.

During my drive, I indulge myself in a pity party. My heavy heart and burdened spirit cry out to God.

Why is life so hard? I can't do this alone. Please lift this burden.

Sunday afternoon, the weatherman forecasts heavy rains. I drive into the city to avoid a messy Monday morning commute. Praise music fills my car, touches something deep inside me, and the tears flow, releasing a torrent of emotions.

Holy Spirit speaks to my heart.

You don't need to carry this burden alone.

I promised to help you.

I am under the load with you.

I understand your heart.

Keep on walking, one step at a time.

Glancing in the rearview mirror, the overcast gloom disappears. I observe a magnificent sunset filling the sky with amazing colors.

The most beautiful sunrises and sunsets occur when the sunlight breaks through the clouds.

I gratefully celebrate God's faithfulness recalling the many times He sustained me through difficult circumstances. Though on this gloomy Sunday afternoon I cannot clearly see His plan, I choose to trust Him for grace to release the burden and take the next step.

I feel His presence urging me forward like a gentle caress.

Holy spirit whispers.

I have your back and I see your future. Trust me.

Prayer of an Abundant Heart

Precious Lord,

I do trust you with all that I am and all that I do.

Help me trust you more.

I cast my cares and doubts on you and implore you to help me endure.

Thank you for carrying me, when I lacked the strength to walk.

Thank you for a beautiful reminder.

The most beautiful skies happen, when the sun breaks through clouds.

Let my life be an example of your light breaking through dark circumstances. I am grateful for your faithfulness.

Personal Reflection

All Wet

God's Word

Therefore, everyone who hears these words of mine and puts them into practice is like a wise man who built his house on the rock. The rain came down, the streams rose, and the winds blew and beat against that house; yet it did not fall, because it had its foundation on the rock. (Matthew 7:24-25 NIV).

Reflection of an Abundant Heart

Wet pavement, some dirt rinsed from an otherwise very dirty car, windshield covered with water – all indications of an overnight rain. Moisture soaked the dry ground. Though the draught-stricken land needed more, the clear sky signaled the end of a much-needed rain event.

Not giving a second thought to the umbrella in the back seat, I headed for the building. The rain stopped. The sky cleared, so why should I carry extra baggage?

In nice weather, the half-mile distance from the employee parking lot to the office provided a pleasant stroll. Two-thirds of the way to the building, intermittent drops fell from the sky. I glanced heavenward at gathering storm clouds.

I quickened my pace. *This isn't too bad. I'll be a little damp but still okay.*

The clouds opened, and rain gushed as if someone turned on a faucet full force. Fear of slick, wet pavement coupled with my recent lack of exercise prevented a mad dash to the building. I half-ran, half-walked the remaining few hundred yards to the door and made my way via the elevator, down the hall and to my desk. I looked as if I stepped out of the shower fully clothed. Drenched, my wet scrubs clung to my skin. Water dripped down my face, smudging the make-up I'd hastily applied earlier. My hair stuck to my head, gummy from gel and hairspray.

One by one my co-workers arrived.

Why wasn't I more like them?

One sat in her car and waited until the deluge passed. Another, unlike me, prepared for the possibility of rain, elected to grab her umbrella. Though caught in the squall, both reached the office dry and perfectly coiffed.

"Don't touch your hair until it dries."

Fortunately, I accepted my friends' wise counsel.

Great. The busiest day of the week and I look like a drowned rat. This puts the bad in bad hair day.

Despite the situation, duty called. The voice of reason in my head shook me from my pity party.

No time to sit around whining about my wet hair and clothes. Eventually everything would dry out.

I refocused and attacked the mountain of charts, reports and messages begging for attention. Soon patients arrived. Hair and clothes almost dry, I borrowed hair spray from a friend, walked down the hall to the bathroom, attempted damage control, and returned to my desk with an attitude adjustment.

Best I could do and as good as it gets.

As the day progressed, almost everyone commented on how good I looked. Several people complimented me on my new hairstyle. I wondered why I spent so much time styling my hair if I got a better look by being more natural. By the end of the day, the storm, a distant memory, seemed no more than a minor inconvenience.

Perhaps my inclination to take life as it comes made me susceptible to sudden storms. Most of the time, I escaped the consequences of being unprepared for rain clouds. Hot, arid days occurred in Texas far more frequently than rainy days. However, those instances when I got caught, proved disastrous.

What if I prepared better?

Why was my umbrella always in the car, or worse yet, at the house?

How could I possibly be prepared all the time for every weather change?

Am I supposed to learn a lesson here?

Hmm? We'll see if I remember the umbrella the next time storm clouds are in the sky, whether or not it is raining.

Perhaps I could avoid future messes.

Like the Texas thunderstorms, storms of life arise suddenly. The phone rings and shatters the peace of an otherwise calm and uneventful day. Unexpected events trigger a sudden squall; job loss, divorce, foreclosure, accidents, illness, frightening test results, death of a loved one. The resulting reaction releases a gambit of emotions for the individual immersed in the crisis.

Crisis effects everyone. Since we can expect tempestuous circumstances, wisdom teaches us to prepare.

How do I react in a crisis?

How can I prepare myself for the sudden storms of life?

Will the principles upon which I build my life allow me to stand strong in any situation?

Jesus instructs us to prepare by building a firm foundation.

Gratefully, we never stand in our own strength.

God's grace sustains and in His power we stand.

Prayer of an Abundant Heart

Oh Lord, My Rock, My Fortress,
I gratefully acknowledge Your presence in my life.
Keep me always close to you.
I seek to know you in the good times.
When the storms of life come, as I know they will,
I only need to speak your name and know You hold and strengthen me.
I desire to stand firm against storms, so others see Your presence in my life.
Make my faith in you so evident that everyone will know You are my sustainer, and my strength comes from You alone.

Personal Reflection

_____

_____

_____

_____

_____

_____

_____

_____

_____

_____

_____

_____

_____

_____

_____

_____

_____

_____

_____

_____

_____

_____

_____

_____

_____

_____

_____

_____

_____

_____

_____

_____

_____

_____

_____

_____

_____

_____

_____

_____

_____

_____

_____

_____

_____

_____.

Sonshine Reflected

God's Word

In him was life, and that life was the light of all mankind. The light shines in the darkness, and the darkness has not overcome it. (John 1: 5-6 NIV).

Reflection of an Abundant Heart

When I thought a sunrise could not be more beautiful, God surprised me with yet another masterpiece. The vibrant sun filled the entire morning sky. The clouds, partially covering the bright yellow-orange sphere, disseminated the rays of the sun. As the rays reflected light behind the clouds, the entire atmosphere illuminated with a burst of radiance. The creator uses clouds to craft the most magnificent sunrises and sunsets.

Whether literal or figurative, we can anticipate storm clouds. We live in a dark and dangerous world. Bad things happen.

Too often, my response to crisis is "Why? What did I do to deserve this?"

One of life's most perplexing dilemmas – Why do bad things happen to good people? Yet our experiences in a broken world teach us to expect struggles. Jesus tells us, *"In this world we will have trouble." (John 16:33 NIV).*

How will we face the reversals and discouragement of this world?

Will we allow problems to overwhelm us?

Will we live under a cloud of disappointment?

Or, will we allow Christ to shine through our situations?

Will we choose to comfort others with the comfort we receive in our struggles?

Though we may never understand why, we can rest in the comfort Holy Spirit provides. God's word promises us His presence. Be strong and courageous.

Do not be afraid or terrified because of them, for the LORD your God goes with you; he will never leave you nor forsake you. (Deuteronomy 31:6 NIV).

Instead of "Why?" perhaps a better question would be "What are You teaching me?" or "How will God bring something good from this pain?"

As I reach out to others dealing with similar circumstances to situations I experience, I find purpose for the struggles.

When sunlight bursts through the clouds in a glorious display of color, streams of light create a glorious reminder to allow God's light to shine in you.

When the "Son" shines through our difficult circumstances, the rays of God's love, like those of the sun breaking through the clouds, disseminate light to a world that desperately needs Him.

Prayer of an Abundant Heart

Lord of comfort,
I pray. Shine through the challenges of my life.
Make me willing to allow every circumstance of my life to be used by you.
Help me to see my problems as opportunities to show your love to others.
My heart is full of gratitude for the beauty you show me daily.
Open my heart to all you have for me.

Personal Reflection

Inner Strength

God's Word

My grace is sufficient for you, for my power is made perfect in weakness. (2 Corinthians 12:9 NIV).

Reflection of an Abundant Heart

The pristine snow covered the drab land like a white blanket. More snow fell in twenty-four hours than most Texans experienced over six decades.

Laden with icy precipitation, the branches of three massive oak trees almost touched the ground.

Television news reported broken limbs and fallen trees caused power outages, and left many people without electricity on the coldest nights of the year.

As I observed the scene in my backyard, I contemplated whether the trees could withstand the weight and additional pressure exerted on their branches.

By midday, the sun came out and melted the snow. The limbs returned to their pre-snow position, appearing as strong as ever.

What makes the difference between trees that break and trees that bend with the pressure but survive just as strong as ever?

Perhaps the depth of their roots or the overall health of the tree allows the trees to continue to thrive despite adverse winds and weather.

Sometimes, like oak trees, we bend under life's

burdens, wondering if we can withstand the weight, or if the next trial may cause us to fracture.

When pressures seem unbearable, our power source remains constant. We can rely on the resources God provides. Even when we lack overall spiritual health or our roots seem a little too shallow, His sustains.

When His children cry, "Help!" He answers, providing what we need when we need it. Deliverance may occur as supernatural miracles, whether we recognize them or not. Often help comes in the form of our family of faith answering Christ's command to bear *one another's burdens.* (*Galatians 6:1-3. NIV*)

Christ serves as our ultimate burden bearer. Holy Spirit comforts with peace beyond human understanding.

No circumstance in life is stronger than our God. No matter what we face, we may bend, but we do not need to fear being broken under our cares.

Rest in this knowledge. His grace is always sufficient.

Prayer of an Abundant Heart

Lord,
You know my struggles. Thank You for the promise never to forsake me.
I rely on Your promise to be with me in any trouble I face.
As I acknowledge my weakness, I tap into Your strength.
Only You provide strength when I am frail.
Help me to rely on this promise, trusting Your sufficient grace.

Personal Reflection

_____

_____

_____

_____

_____

_____

_____

_____

_____

_____

_____

_____

_____

_____

_____

_____

_____

_____

_____

_____

_____

_____

_____

_____

_____

_____

_____

_____

Hot and Dry

God's Word

The Spirit and the bride say, "Come! And let him who hears say, Come! Whoever is thirsty let him come and whoever wishes let him take the free gift of the water of life. (Revelation 22:17 NIV).

Reflections of an Abundant Heart

The memory of spring rains, filling ponds to overflowing and saturating lawns, faded quickly in the hot, dry summer. Two months earlier, deluges caused muddy fields and soggy yards, too wet to mow. However, things dry out quickly in the scorching heat of the Texas sun. In contrast to the brilliant colors of spring, the hot, arid summers produced conditions almost as brown and dead as in the winter.

Farmers irrigated fields to produce crops. Gardeners watered regularly so the lawns and flowers decorating their landscapes remained green and beautiful. Landscapers chose plants for the ability to survive in hot, dry climates. We educated ourselves in methods of caring for our investments. All too often I walked out my back door and saw my flowers drooping from too much heat and not enough water. Left alone, they would wither and die.

Like the plants our bodies must have water to carry out the functions necessary to sustain life. If the body loses more fluid than it takes in, dehydration occurs with serious consequences. Just like plants, if humans fail to replace fluids they will die. Dietary and health experts suggest six to eight glasses of water a day to maintain the appropriate fluid balance.

Most of us choose to drink all kinds of fluids, including coffee, tea, or sodas, but not nearly enough water. Most weight loss diets encourage drinking water and minimizing the other liquids. Curiously, the more I drink, the more I want. I actually get thirsty for water.

The same principles apply to my spiritual life.

Society offers alternatives to fill the hunger and thirst of my soul. These pursuits may satisfy temporarily but cannot replace the living water necessary for spiritual nourishment. As I spend time with God in scripture and prayer, my spirit thirsts for God's word and for communion with Him. The more I learn, the more I want to learn. As I draw nearer to Christ, the more I want to experience Him. I cannot get enough.

Fortunately, the nourishment I require is plentiful. Its source is unlimited. The spirit invites us to come and be satisfied with an endless supply of living water.

Prayer of an Abundant Heart

Sustainer, Source of all life,
Thank You for the promise to quench my thirst with an endless supply of Your spirit.
Help me to be faithful in my quest for the Word and Your presence.
I can only experience Your unconditional promise when I draw near You.
Help me pay attention. Fill my spirit so I can live nourished, hydrated and healthy.

Personal Reflection

_____

_____

_____

_____

_____

_____

_____

_____

_____

_____

_____

_____

_____

_____

_____

_____

_____

_____

_____

_____

_____

_____

_____

_____

_____

_____

_____

_____

Devastating Storms

God's Word

These words I speak to you are not incidental additions to your life, homeowner improvements to your standard of living. They are foundational words, words to build a life on. If you work these words out in your life, you are like a smart carpenter who built his house on a solid rock. Rain poured down, the river flooded, a tornado hit — but nothing moved that house. It was fixed to the rock. (Matthew 7:24-25 The Message).

Reflections of an Abundant Heart

Tornadoes historically ravage Texas and Oklahoma, often destroying entire communities. The designation of "tornado alley" refers to a specific area where devastating storms frequently occur. Though Texans live with the threat of inclement weather, nature's storms, not limited to one geographic location, happen throughout the world.

Tornadoes and strong winds pique my curiosity. One storm leaves an entire community in rubble. Another odd phenomenon leaves one house demolished and the house next door unscathed.

Television news and the internet make the world a much smaller place. Our hearts break as we observe the pain of victims of earthquakes, fires, floods, or storms around the world. I shed tears for people who lose all material possessions and sometimes those they love. They struggle through the shock yet somehow find the resilience and will to rebuild.

Life's storms, much like the winds devastating communities and homes, strike without warning. Tragedies, threatening to knock us down and out, take many forms. Perhaps the storm begins with a visit to the doctor and devastating health news. The voice on the other end of the phone line delivers a report of an accident. The dreaded "pink slip" announces a lay off with all the financial upheaval job losses entail.

Suddenly and unexpectedly, we find ourselves in the middle of a raging storm. Just like actual storms, life's squalls seldom involve one person. The ripple effect spreads through family, friends and community.

Scripture instructs us to live wisely. It admonishes us to make sure we build on a strong, solid foundation – one that will withstand the storm.

Even when the squalls of life take the entire structure of our lives, the foundation remains and leaves something upon which to rebuild.

Prayer of an Abundant Heart
Master of the Storm and the Wind,
Help me always trust you in the storms of my life.
The winds and the waves are calmed with one word from you.
Remind me that you are the solid foundation on which I must build my life.
When I observe the storms in the lives of others, please use me as a witness to your power and a resource on which they can rely.
Help my life always to point to you as the anchor and the stronghold in any trouble.

Personal Reflection

_____

_____

_____

_____

_____

_____

_____

_____

_____

_____

_____

_____

_____

_____

_____

_____

_____

_____

_____

_____

_____

_____

_____

_____

_____

_____

Stand Firm

God's Word

Therefore, put on the full armor of God, so that when the day of evil comes, you may be able to stand your ground, and after you have done everything, to stand. (Ephesians 6:13 NIV).

Reflection of an Abundant Heart

My natural sleep pattern encourages night owl behavior. I prefer sleeping in to rising early. Ironically, I enjoy early morning commutes.

Pulling out of my driveway onto a dark road, I look to the eastern sky to assure myself that the morning star still shines brightly. Unless obscured by fog or nasty weather, I can count on seeing it every day. Whether I see it or not, it still performs its function in the morning sky.

I admit my lack of interest in the science of astronomy, so it surprises me to learn what we refer to as the morning and the evening star isn't really a star at all. Rather, the planet Venus provides the bright light in the morning and evening sky. Not caring whether Venus is a star or a planet, I consistently observe a ritual of searching the sky for the heavenly body which outshines the stars around it and rises even when no other stars appear in the sky. It reliably occupies an assigned place and serves as a compass.

The world needs a compass. Standing firm for faith points others to our true compass—Jesus Christ.

Twenty-first century society constantly admonishes

us to be politically correct in our speech and attitudes. While we all need lessons of tolerance, love, and acceptance, it is essential that we know what we believe and stand for our principles.

As a young adult, my minister and friend, Dan Griffin, significantly influenced my life. He often encouraged us to stand firm with this mantra, "Wrong is wrong, even if everybody is doing it. And right is right, even if no one is doing it."

Our text book is the Bible. Our standard is Christ, who declared, *I, Jesus, have sent my angel to give you this testimony for the churches. I am the Root and the Offspring of David, and the bright Morning Star. (Revelations 22:16 NIV).*

Prayer of An Abundant Heart
Lord Jesus,
Thank you for your example of standing firm.
Thank you for the consistency of nature, for the reliability of the skies which remind me, You never change.
You remain the same today, tomorrow and forever.
Give me the courage of my convictions to stand for what is right, even when I must stand alone.

Personal Reflection

_____

_____

_____

_____

_____

_____

Raging Waters

God's Word
The men were amazed and asked, "What kind of man is this? Even the winds and the waves obey him!" (Mathew 8:27 NIV).

Reflection of an Abundant Heart

Same day—same bridge—same body of water, tumultuous water raged replacing the glassy surface observed hours earlier. The strong wind currents created white-capping waves on the small lake.

What a difference a few hours and a little wind made in conditions of the lakes and rivers! Sudden changes in weather conditions turned a peaceful fishing trip into a struggle for survival. The safety of the dock seemed far away.

Unusually heavy spring rains transformed gently flowing streams into powerfully rushing rivers with fast-moving currents. Signs cautioned visitors to stay out of the river. Despite the warnings, a few dare devils tempted fate. Thrill seekers found the thrilling challenge worth the risk. The news reported the drowning of one for whom the danger proved fatal.

The gospels of Matthew and Luke recorded such a tempest. As Jesus and His disciples started across the lake, the calm water forecasted no warning of the pending disturbance. Totally unprepared, the little group faced a violent storm threatening to sink their boat.

Unconcerned and fatigued from the day's work, Jesus

43

slept soundly in the bottom of the boat until His followers woke him with fearful cries of "Save Us! We are about to drown!"

Christ first rebuked their lack of faith. Then he rebuked the winds and the waves and the sea instantly calmed.

Many situations result from our own poor choices or rash decisions. If we ignore warning signs or rebel, we face consequences. We behave from a position of self-reliance only to realize our limitations. Other times perils occur as a condition of living on earth.

When life's unexpected storms threaten my peace of mind, like the disciples I cry out, "Lord, don't you care that I am in distress? Can't you see that I am about to be destroyed."

He responds in the middle of my predicament.

Sometimes He rebukes the situation and rescues me.

More often, He calms my anxious heart and assures me that together we will weather any crisis I must face.

Prayer of an Abundant Heart

Lord, Jesus Christ,
You are stronger than any circumstance I will ever face.
I trust you to lead me through any trial placed in my path.
I never want to hear you say,
"You of little faith; why are you so afraid."
When I must face a storm, calm my spirit and give me the strength to stand firm.
Help me to live in confidence and assurance.
No matter what situation I must face, You Walk through it with me.
Thank You, Lord, for this promise.

Personal Reflection

_____

_____

_____

_____

_____

_____

_____

_____

_____

_____

_____

_____

_____

_____

_____

_____

_____

_____

_____

_____

_____

_____

_____

_____

The Eye of God

God's Word

Are not two sparrows sold for a penny? Yet not one of them will fall to the ground outside your Father's care. And even the very hairs of your head are all numbered. So don't be afraid; you are worth more than many sparrows. (Matthew 10:29-31 NIV).

Reflection of an Abundant Heart

Living in two worlds offers a distinction between the urgent velocity of the city. Compare the rush from one destination to another with the quiet unhurried pace of leisurely walking on a country lane. I happily welcome the divergence from hasty commutes and a demanding job to a peaceful stroll in a quiet country neighborhood. The noise of city streets contrasts sharply with the sounds of birds chirping and leaves rustling in the breeze.

The slow, steady ascent to the top of the hill always leaves me breathless. The really steep incline and a lack of physical fitness results in significant dyspnea. Stopping to catch my breath, I gaze into the skies. My imagination flows freely, and I revisit a practice from childhood. What shapes do the clouds form?

The vision leaves me more breathless than the strenuous work out. Without a doubt, I see it! The clouds form the shape of an eye – the lid, the brow and from the center, the sun forms a fiery iris and pupil.

I reflect on a favorite hymn, *His Eye Is on the Sparrow,*

and contemplate the inspiration for the lyrics. Civilla Dufree Martin, a teacher with modest musical training, and her husband, Walter, a Harvard trained musician, often collaborated on hymn compositions.

Early in the spring of 1905, the couple formed a deep friendship with the Doolittles. Mr. and Mrs. Doolittle suffered physical limitations confining her to bed and him to a wheelchair. Despite their afflictions, they lived happy Christian lives which inspired and comforted all who knew them. During one visit, the Martins asked the secret of contentment in such difficult circumstances. Mrs. Doolittle simply replied. *"His eye is on the sparrow, and I know He watches me."*

This expression of faith sparked the imagination of the composers. Civilla and Walter wrote the words of comfort which continue to be sung over 100 years later.

His Eye Is on the Sparrow
Civilla Martin

Why should I feel discouraged?
Why should the shadows come?
Why should my heart be lonely,
and long for heaven and home?
When Jesus is my portion,
My constant friend is he,
His eye is on the sparrow
and I know he watches me.

Fast forward several years from my stroll to the top of the hill. I scroll my Facebook feed. A friend posts a photo of the sky. Several people see futuristic space ships. Not me. I see an image in the clouds. A face with prominent eyes watches the world below.

I imagine myself in the loving gaze of my Heavenly Father.

Nothing escapes God's attention. He carefully observes each of us as we walk through our daily routines. We are never out of His sight; not when we breathlessly climb to the top of a hill, not as we rest and recharge for the tasks that lie ahead, not as we busy ourselves with mundane tasks of daily living, and not when we experience crisis.

He remains ever present—always watching, loving, and caring.

Prayer of an Abundant Heart
Abba, Father,
Thank you for your amazing care for me.
Thank you that you see every joy, every care, every struggle, every moment of my life.
Keep me aware of all the ways you watch over me, protect me and surround me with your love.

Personal Reflection

_____

_____

_____

_____

_____

_____

_____

_____

_____

_____

Restoration by Still Waters

God's Word

The Lord is my shepherd. I shall not want. He makes me lie down in green pastures. He leads me beside still waters. He restores my soul. (Psalm 23:1-2 NIV).

Reflection of an Abundant Heart

Most Americans spend a minimum of eight hours a day at an office or other place of employment. An additional two hours spent in the car getting to and from work, time for grocery shopping, laundry and chores necessary to keep a home in livable condition add to cumulative time constraints. Remaining competent in a chosen profession requires continuing education. Doctors advise at least twenty minutes of exercise a day, as well as eight hours of sleep each night. A quick tally totals approximately twenty hours of a twenty-four-hour day. This fails to take into consideration family, community or church responsibilities, and leaves limited time to pursue hobbies like reading, writing, knitting, singing or playing an instrument. No wonder I find myself feeling overwhelmed and exhausted.

Considering the chaotic pace of life, my heart pounds. I am not designed to live this way.

God wants better for me.

In His wisdom, He commands me to rest.

Remember the Sabbath day by keeping it holy. Six days you shall labor and do all your work, but the seventh day is a sabbath to the Lord your God. On it you shall not do any work, neither you, nor your son or daughter, not your male or female servant, not your animals. Nor any foreigner residing in your towns. For in six days the LORD made the heavens and the earth, the sea and all that is in them, but he rested on the seventh day. Therefore, the LORD blessed the Sabbath day and made it holy. (Exodus 20: 8-11 NIV).

Though the science books say water covers about three fourths of the earth's surface, the experience of most Texans might dispute this fact. It takes some effort to find a body of water. The scarcity of natural water ways makes me especially appreciative of the lakes on my regular route.

During one hectic season of my life, Lake Granbury captured my attention. That evening no wind disturbed its glassy smooth surface. Quiet and calm, it beckoned me to come sit by the shore. Stop the hectic pace and rest if only for a minute.

In a rush to get home, I ignored the invitation.

None of my pursuits is fundamentally wrong. To the contrary, each, kept in proper prospective, provides a necessary purpose. However, when I fail to recognize God's invitation to spend time alone with Him, I miss what He wants to say through His Word and through the lessons He teaches me in quiet times of reflection.

Sometimes I sit beside a bubbling stream, a calm lake, or on the shore of the ocean, listening to the rhythmic sound of the rolling waves. Other times, I seek renewal in another setting of nature. Any place quiet enough to listen for God to speak provides opportunities for restoration.

Wherever I practice the discipline of reading God's word and communicating my heart to Him in prayer, my soul receives the rest I need.

An often-quoted phrase "still waters run deep" refers to a calm appearing person with considerable inner emotion, character, or intellect.

If this is true of mortal man, imagine the deep truths God wants to reveal as we sit quietly by the streams of still waters. After all, the Psalmist said our Lord leads us there.

Prayer of an Abundant Heart

Lord, who is my shepherd,
I treasure the quiet time I spend with you.
Forgive me when I fail to make this time a priority.
I crave the rest and nourishment you alone can give.
No one and nothing else can provide restoration for my soul.
Thank you for the invitation to come away from the hurried pace of life and sit with you beside still waters.
My response is "Yes."
Consider this my RSVP.
I will meet you to receive everything necessary to fulfill Your purpose for me.

Personal Reflection

_____

_____

_____

_____

_____

_____

_____

_____

_____

_____

Stay Alert

God's Word

Be alert and of sober mind. Your enemy the devil prowls around like a roaring lion looking for someone to devour. Resist him, standing firm in the faith, because you know that the family of believers throughout the world is undergoing the same kind of sufferings. And the God of all grace, who called you to his eternal glory in Christ, after you have suffered a little while, will himself restore you and make you strong, firm and steadfast. (1 Peter 5: 8-10 NIV).

Reflections of an Abundant Heart

Mama deer and her twin babies visit our backyard almost nightly. Fascinated by their behavior, I love to sit quietly and observe. As long as I remain still and quiet, they graze contentedly.

Deer possess both short- and long-term memory and utilize this skill to find food and water and to navigate potential danger. The maturity of Mama Deer hones her memory and prepares her to protect herself and the fawns. Her keen senses of sight, sound, and smell instinctively assure her. These humans present no threat.

She and her twin fawns graze peacefully. The oak trees provide a steady source of acorns and cool shade. The consistent supply keeps them returning each evening.

At the slightest sound, Mama snaps to attention. On hyperalert with ears pointed and eyes widened, she assesses any potential danger. She either returns to grazing or bolts if necessary. The fawns, still sporting their spots, take cues from their mother. As long as she grazes peacefully, so do they. If she runs, they follow.

Natural predators, coyotes and mountain lions, lurk and present real danger. Though prohibited in our subdivision on nearby acreage, hunters may pose a threat. Mama Deer needs to be on high alert. The doe and fawns' survival depend on her acute senses. Observing the maternal habits of the deer family causes me to reflect on scripture. In his letter to the Ephesians, the apostle Paul admonishes,

Take the helmet of salvation and the sword of the Spirit, which is the word of God. And pray in the Spirit on all occasions with all kinds of prayers and requests. With this in mind, be alert and always keep on praying for all the Lord's people. (Ephesians 6:17-18 NIV).

Like coyotes and mountain lions stalk deer, Satan prowls the earth, looking to pounce on our weaknesses. When we complacently fail to arm and protect ourselves, we become vulnerable to attacks of the enemy.

Be alert! Like Mama Deer, at the first sound of danger, snap to attention. Keenly be aware of any threat. Access the danger and flee if necessary.

Prayer of an Abundant Heart

Holy Spirit,
Guard my heart and mind.
Keep me alert to anything threatening to divert my attention from spiritual concerns.
Tether my heart with my brothers and sisters in God's family, and protect us from the attacks of Satan.
Remind me to daily put on the whole armor of God so that I can stand firm against the forces of evil in this world.

Personal Reflection

_____

_____

_____

_____

_____

_____

_____

_____

_____

_____

_____

_____

_____

_____

_____

_____

_____

_____

_____

_____

_____

_____

_____

_____

_____

_____

Night Lights

God's Word
Praise be to the God and Father of our Lord Jesus Christ, the Father of compassion and the God of all comfort, who comforts us in all our troubles, so that we can comfort those in any trouble with the comfort we ourselves receive from God. (2 Corinthians 1:3-4 NIV).

Reflection of an Abundant Heart
At least one night a week, the commute required driving in the dark. Fatigued, sometimes near exhaustion, the long drive to my country home served as time to decompress from the stress of a long work week. As I drove home, I often used the time to focus on lights—the lights of the cities of Dallas and Fort Worth, the lights of Granbury, the lights of Bluff Dale. What did those lights represent?

Are the lights of businesses intended to beckon customers?

Yes, we are still here, come on in. We're open late and we will still be happy for you to spend your money with us.

Other companies advertised.

Come back later and bring your business. We are closed but will be happy to serve you when we return.

Still others kept lights burning to light the night and deter theft or vandalism.

However, the business lights failed to capture my attention.

Lights shining from houses along my route captivated

me. Illumination from windows represented homes and the families living in them. Late at night, when most everyone else slept, why did those lights still shine? What kept the inhabitants awake? My imagination ran free. Maybe the lights celebrated an event. Some good news created too much excitement for the family to sleep. Perhaps a new baby arrived and needed to be fed in the middle of the night. Maybe a light represented someone taking advantage of quiet time to work on a project needing undivided attention. Was there a party happening? Was someone in the house ill? Was a parent waiting for a rebellious teenager to come home safely? Could the concerns of life cause a restless night?

There could be endless reasons for sleeplessness; health, finances, relationships, loneliness.

Why do I care about these lights and the issues they represent?

In Luke 13:34 Jesus expressed concern over the city of Jerusalem. He longed to gather them together and care for them.

As Christians, aren't we called to have that same concern?

Scripture admonishes us to show compassion to others, and reach them with the gospel of Christ. They will only be reached if we as Christians care about their deepest concerns.

How can we fulfill this calling unless we make ourselves available?

We all go through difficult times in our lives. The lessons you or I learn in a hard time may be exactly what is needed to encourage someone else.

I really want to be that kind of encourager. How about you?

Prayer of an Abundant Heart

Father God.
Open my eyes to recognize the needs around me.
Put someone in my life that needs me to walk beside them.
Lead me to those who need to learn from experiences I faced.
Allow me to show the same compassion to others you showed me in the hard times of my life.
I make myself available to you.
Use me to show your love and compassion to those I meet daily.

Personal Reflection

_____

_____

_____

_____

_____

_____

_____

_____

_____

_____

_____

_____

_____

_____

_____

Royal Colors of Morning

God's Word

Therefore, God exalted him to the highest place and gave him the name that is above every name, that at the name of Jesus every knee should bow, in heaven and on earth and under the earth, and that every tongue should confess that Jesus Christ is Lord, to the glory of God the Father. (Philippians 2:9-11 NIV).

Reflection of an Abundant Heart

The reward of an early morning commute—an indigo sky—the predominate hue of the morning's dawn. As the rich, violet blue color reflected light of the sunrise, the sky came alive with color. Multiple shades of blue, pink and purple accented by the scattered white of the clouds welcomed the sun as it introduced golden rays.

The magnificent sky exclaims,

Look and see!

Reflect and understand!

Observe the colors of royalty, purple robes and a crown of gold.

Recognize your King!

Who is King of my life?

Who is King of your life?

In the midst of a worship service, we acknowledge the Lordship of Christ. Then we rush headlong into the work week. When life's demands clamor for attention, do we forget who is King?

Everything in creation reminds us, God is in control

and He is our King.

The Bible tells us that one day everyone will acknowledge the Lordship of Jesus Christ.

If Christ appeared and split the sky today, would our reaction be shock and surprise rather than awe and recognition of the King's return to claim his loyal subjects?

Jesus told us to be ready. At that time, they will see the Son of Man coming in a cloud with power and great glory. *When these things begin to take place, stand up and lift up your heads, because your redemption is drawing near. (Luke 21:27-29 NIV).*

Prayer of an Abundant Heart

Christ Jesus,
I recognize my inability to control even the simplest of tasks.
I ask you to use me to be your hands to serve a hurting world.
Indwell my heart each moment. Be the Lord and Master of my life.
Take Your rightful place as King.
When I observe the royal colors of morning, remind me to anticipate Your return.

Personal Reflection

_____

_____

_____

_____

_____

_____

_____

Total Eclipse

God's Word

This is what the LORD says, he who appoints the sun to shine by day, who decrees the moon and stars to shine by night, who stirs up the sea so that its waves roar – the LORD Almighty is his name. (Jeremiah 31:35 NIV).

Reflection of an Abundant Heart

The *American Heritage Dictionary* defines an eclipse as the partial or complete obscuring of one celestial body by another. A lunar eclipse occurs when the sun, earth and moon perfect align with the earth in the middle and can only occur when there is a full moon.

One August morning, in the hours just before dawn, a total lunar eclipse appeared in the north Texas sky. The full moon, covered by a shadow of red, offered only a rim of its usual light. The overall effect resulted in a darker morning than usual as the earth obscured the normally bright light of the moon. The stars, however, shined brighter than usual, as they no longer competed with the moon to light the night sky.

Eclipse may also be defined as a decline into obscurity, disuse or disgrace. As I observed the eclipse during my morning commute, I pondered the things eclipsing the source of light and joy in my life. Each day introduces a myriad of circumstances that if allowed may eclipse joy. Perhaps the obstruction is an illness or accident, the death of a loved one, the end of a relationship, financial or career concerns, or even personal insecurities.

Consider the difference between happiness and joy. The emotion of happiness depends on circumstances. Joy recognizes an abiding hope and faith that God can be trusted with the details of my future.

The lunar eclipse happened for a brief moment in time. If you failed to be in the right place at the right time, you missed the event.

A favorite phrase used by our household applies to both joys and sorrows, "and it came to pass" which means "it did not come to stay!"

In the great scheme of things, earthly troubles are brief. Looking back, I often wonder, why I waste so much time and energy fretting over a difficult circumstance. I never regret the times I release the circumstance, whether trivial or grim. As I divert my attention away from obstructions and focus on the blessings of my life, God's light shines brighter. He restores my joy.

Prayer of an Abundant Heart

Heavenly Father, Maker of the Sun, Moon and Stars,
Keep my heart fixed on you and your provision.
Divert my attention from the obstructions.
You have blessed me beyond comprehension and I praise you.
Help me to view the difficulties in my life as opportunities
to grow closer to you and better understand who I am in you.

Personal Reflection

_____

_____

_____

_____

_____

_____

_____

_____

_____

_____

_____

_____

_____

_____

_____

_____

_____

_____

_____

_____

_____

_____

Full Moon

God's Word

LORD, our Lord,
how majestic is your name in all the earth!
You have set your glory in the heavens.
Through the praise of children and infants
You have established a stronghold against Your
enemies, to silence the foe and the avenger.
When I consider Your heavens, the work of Your
fingers, the moon and the stars,
which You have set in place,
what is mankind that You are mindful of them?
human beings that You care for them?
You have made them a little lower than the angels
and crowned them with glory and honor.
You made them rulers over the works of Your hands;
You put everything under their feet:
all flocks and herds,
and the animals of the wild,
the birds in the sky,
and the fish in the sea,
all that swim the paths of the seas.
LORD, our Lord,
how majestic is Your name in all the earth!
(Psalm 8 NIV).

Reflection of an Abundant Heart

An incredibly beautiful orb of light filled the evening sky in stark contrast to the totally eclipsed one of the same day's dawn. Gazing into the heavens, I reflected on the many connotations associated with this phase of the moon.

Many movies portray the full moon as a precursor to evil events, like attacks by werewolves or vampires. Some people stare at the night sky trying to recognize the face of a man in the moon. Lovers gaze longingly at the night sky, finding it romantically captivating.

Lunar months measure pregnancy, and many people believe the changes in the moon's cycle may signal labor to begin for an expectant mother. My very unscientific nursing observation supports that people are much more emotional when the moon is full. Often my medical colleagues quip, "There must be a full moon. The crazies are out."

From werewolves, to romance, to emotional upheaval, to new babies on the way there is a fascination with the moon. Scientist and astronauts, curious enough to visit, came back with reports. My generation remembers watching television with rapt attention as Neil Armstrong walked on the lunar surface.

Just like the sun, the moon is constant. We watch the cycles. New moons and full moons guide our calendar. The more we know; the more creation fascinates us.

God placed the sun, moon, and stars in place. He controls the orbits and keeps them in heavenly order. I stand in amazement of creation and marvel at the beauty of each sunrise, sunset, and night sky. Wonder of all wonders—the God of the Universe is mindful of me!

Prayer of an Abundant Heart

Creator of the Universe
I praise you for the beauty of your handiwork, for the awesome night skies.
I am thankful for Your faithfulness.
When I am overwhelmed by my responsibilities, I am humbled to think that you hold the world together with just a word.
I am amazed that you love and care for me, despite my shortcomings.
I truly stand in awe of you.
O LORD, my Lord,
how majestic is Your name in all the earth!

Personal Reflection

_____

_____

_____

_____

_____

_____

_____

_____

_____

_____

_____

_____

_____

History and Symbols of Advent

God's Word

When Jesus spoke again to the people, he said, "I am the light of the world. Whoever follows me will never walk in darkness, but will have the light of life." (John 8: 12 NIV).

Reflection of an Abundant Heart

I love everything about Christmas—the music, lights, decoration, food, presents and family traditions. I especially enjoy the celebration of Advent. I first learned about the practice of Advent as a young mother and incorporated it as a family tradition.

Over the years, I participated without knowing or understanding the history, significance, and symbolism of Advent. Learning the history and traditions deepens my appreciation for the celebration.

Our family decorates the dining room table with an Advent Wreath and light candles each Sunday. We light Advent Candles both at church and at home, incorporating scripture or devotional thoughts.

The word advent originates from the Latin *Adventus,* meaning coming or arrival. Most traditions recognize advent as a time of anticipation and expectation of the birth of Christ.

71

Advent began as early as the Fourth century as a time of fasting and prayer for new Christians, first mentioned in the 300's A.D. at the Council of Saragosa. It gradually developed into a season that stretched across the month of December. The season lasts for four Sundays leading up to Christmas and serves as a time of spiritual preparation to celebrate the birth of Christ. Some traditions still observe fasting and prayer. Our celebration not only symbolizes waiting for Christ's birth but also His final return.

The roots of modern Advent celebrations stretch back to 16th century Germany. In 1839, Lutheran theologian and social activist, Johann Hinrich Wichern, opened Das Rauh Haus (Rough House) for wayward men and boys in Hamburg, Germany. He enlisted local, volunteer teachers to train the residents as tradesmen so they could make a living. Surrounded by young boys who constantly asked, "Is it Christmas yet?" Wichern found a practical way to avoid the daily question as well as adding a spiritual element.

He created a candle wheel from a wagon/cart wheel and hung it in the Rough House prayer room. He filled the original wreath with four large white candles and twenty smaller red ones. Each weekday and Saturday he lit one of the red candles. On each Sunday, he lit a white Candle. By Christmas, all the candles burned brightly.

The custom soon spread to homes in surrounding villages, as well as Protestant and Catholic churches throughout the region. Wichern likely used red and white candles because their availability. They remain the traditional color in the Lutheran and Anglican Churches. Once the tradition spread, pastors and priests used the four candles to represent the themes of the Advent season. They adopted and adapted the colors of purple, pink and white.

Colors of Advent signify the themes of Christmas. Red symbolizes communion and Jesus' blood and sacrifice. Purple signifies prayer and penance, as well as the color of royalty. The rose candle denotes joy. White represents purity and light

Each layer of symbolism represented in the Advent wreath, encourages us to focus on an aspect of the Christmas story. The circular shape represents the eternal nature of God, His infinite love for us and the eternal life we find in Jesus. Evergreens symbolize the continuity of life. Holly, with spikey leaves represent the crown of thorns and the red berries remind us of Jesus blood and sacrifice.

The candles shine brightly in the midst of darkness, symbolizing Jesus who came as Light into our dark world. We light the center candle on Christmas Eve or Christmas Day to celebrate Jesus' birth and to remind us He is coming again.

Jesus came to a dark world, not unlike the society we encounter. He still illuminates our lives and commissions us to share that light with those who struggle in darkness.

Prayer of an Abundant Heart

Jesus, Light of the World,

Ignite the flame within me, so others will see the motivation for all I do and glorify You.

Renew the passion for sharing Your love and light.

Keep me focused on Your light, not only during the season of advent but throughout the year.

Personal Reflection

_____

_____

_____

_____

_____

_____

_____

_____

_____

_____

_____

_____

_____

_____

_____

_____

Keep the Flame Burning

God's Word

You are the light of the world. A town built on a hill cannot be hidden. Neither do people light a lamp and put it under a bowl. Instead, they put it on its stand, and it gives light to everyone in the house. In the same way, let your light shine before others, that they may see your good deeds and glorify your Father in heaven. (Matthew 5:14-16 NIV).

Reflection of an Abundant Heart

Each year our small rural churches host a community candlelight service. Typically occurring the Sunday prior to Christmas, the tradition dates back more than a half century.

The candles from the advent wreath serve to illuminate the sanctuary, representing Christ as the source of light to a dark world. Christmas 2024, the pastor lit a candle from the Christ Candle and passed the light to the candles of the participants while we sang "Silent Night." Before lighting the candles, he instructed us to carry our candles out the door into the darkness of the evening as a visual representation of our mandate to carry Jesus' light into a dark world.

He intended us to carry our candles out into the night

and around to the fellowship hall where a feast of Christmas treats waited.

I stood at the front of the church, and bill witnessed the worshippers as they exited. Many of the candles burned out before they reached the back door. Others were purposefully snuffed out and placed in a basket on a table at the door. Some made it outside, but the wind quickly blew out the flame. Few lasted long enough to make any impact on the darkness.

Christ is the Light of the world. He commanded us to go and tell. People walking in darkness desperately need the hope we have to share.

Satan conspires to extinguish the Light.

I can only shine for Jesus by keeping the candle burning brightly. Yet, sometimes I fail to keep it ignited. The world wants to douse my light. Apathy causes me to snuff it out before I leave the building. Sometimes it flickers when gusts of pain, suffering, and grief cause me to doubt my source of strength and light. Evil winds threaten to blow out my candle.

Jesus admonishes us to carry the light to a world desperately in need of Him. He calls us to illuminate the way to the feast, which I trust will be far greater than any banquet we can imagine.

Prayer of an Abundant Heart

Christ of Christmas, Emmanuel, God with us,
Thank you for coming to bring light into a dark world.
We have no hope apart from you. I want to obey your command.
Forgive me when I allow anything to dim the flame.
In the words of a song I learned as a child, I pray,
"Give me oil in my lamp, keep me burning until the break of day."
(public domain)

Personal Reflection

_____

_____

_____

_____

_____

_____

_____

_____

_____

_____

_____

_____

_____

_____

Peace Beyond Human Understanding

God's Word

And the peace of God, which transcends all understanding, will guard your hearts and your minds in Christ Jesus. (Philippians 4:7 NIV).

Reflection of an Abundant Heart

We wasted several minutes attempting to assess the problem and decide the appropriate course of action.

"Are you okay? Talk to me! Tell me what's happening!" I spoke with an uncommon urgency in my voice.

"Something's not right. The dizziness is getting worse."

My husband staggered as he struggled back to his recliner.

He'd experienced these spells with increasing frequency over the past few days, but this one seemed different, lasting longer.

My nursing observation skills kicked in and the questions flooded in a steady stream. Tell me your name. What day is it? Who's the president? Where are you?

Though he answered appropriately, my gut told me we urgently needed help.

The question of whether to wait for the symptoms to pass answered itself as things rapidly deteriorated.

Next decision – call an ambulance and wait 30 minutes for them to arrive or get in the car and deliver him to the hospital emergency room 30 minutes away.

Can you walk to the car with my help?

I think so.

Let's go.

On the drive to the hospital, I kept talking to him. The responses continued to be appropriate if somewhat slowed.

Arriving in record time, I left him in the car, rushed into the emergency room, and announced loudly. "I need help, NOW! My husband is either having a seizure or a stroke!"

An attendant with a wheelchair accompanied me to the car and wheeled Kerry to an intake room where a nurse waited to access his symptoms. I relayed medical history and a medication list.

One of the medical team escorted me to a chair in the hallway. With an unobstructed view of the treatment room, I watched as the team prepared to shock my husband's heart back into a normal rhythm. I understood all too well what was about to happen.

The nurse explained, "I'm going to give you a dose of Fentanyl for pain."

Kerry's eyes widened, "Isn't that the drug that's killing people?

"Well, we got a really good batch," the nurse joked.

"But I'm not having any pain."

"You are about to."

A moment of quiet. Then I hear, "CLEAR" followed by a blood-curdling scream.

During the fifty plus years of our marriage, I developed coping skills as we faced more than our share of medical challenges. Friends and family described me as calm and collected in the midst of crises. The crumbling mess of emotions always occurred after the crisis passed.

Sidelined, without any illusion of control or a role to play in the current crisis, I did the only thing I knew worked. I sincerely prayed for Kerry's health and heart. I pled for comfort and strength to face the next moments.

I received exactly what I needed. PEACE.

The gift of peace came first. The medical intervention resulted in a restoration of normal heart rhythm, and life continued with some major lifestyle changes. The result could have been very different.

I felt Holy Spirit embrace me and calm the anxiety. My spirit knew. No matter the outcome, we would be okay.

Every personal storm differs. Only those who experience the peace and calm Holy Spirit provides when their world falls apart fully understand.

I love the way scripture assures me of this kind of peace under fire.

Don't fret or worry. Instead of worrying, pray. Let petitions and praises shape your worries into prayers, letting God know your concerns. Before you know it, a sense of God's wholeness, everything coming together for good, will come and settle you down. It's wonderful what happens when Christ displaces worry at the center of your life. (Philippians 4:6-7 The Message).

Life on earth presents challenges. We live in a broken world. However, we possess a source to combat the fear and anxiety of losing control.

Don't fret. Don't worry. Pray.

Rest in the assurance God hears and provides.

Practice in times of ease so it will be second nature when the crisis comes.

Prayer of an Abundant Heart

Father God, Lord Jesus, Holy Spirit,

Thank you for the assurance of peace no matter the storm. I release control over any situation.

I rely on the promise of your presence as I navigate problems of broken bodies, broken health, and a broken world.

I eagerly wait for the day You bring restoration. I praise You in every circumstance.

Personal Reflection

_____

_____

_____

_____

_____

_____

_____

_____

_____

_____

_____

_____

_____

_____

_____

_____

Firm Foundation; Then What

God's Word

And whoever does not carry their cross and follow me cannot be my disciple. Suppose one of you wants to build a tower. Won't you first sit down and estimate the cost to see if you have enough money to complete it? For if you lay the foundation and are not able to finish it, everyone who sees it will ridicule you, saying, 'This person began to build and wasn't able to finish. (Luke 14:27-30 NIV).

Reflection of an Abundant Heart

The signs appeared subtly. First, a fine crack spread from the top of a closet door to the corner. Then a more noticeable one crept above the bathroom door jam. Doors throughout the house either stuck in the closed position or wouldn't shut without being forced. Though patching and repainting provided a temporary fix, the cracks quickly reappeared. Obviously, we needed professional help to correct the source of the problem, a fault in our foundation.

This house held so many precious memories—holidays, birthdays, anniversaries, hosting friends and family. We expected it to be our forever home and sure didn't want it to crumble around us.

Everything about it screamed 1977, from the galley kitchen with harvest gold appliances and bright orange, yellow, and green wallpaper to the bright yellow floors and countertops. The avocado green shag carpet completed the vibe. By the time cracks appeared, it needed updating to reflect the 1990's. Facing the prospect of an expensive repair, it seemed like a good time for a refresh. Armed with estimated cost of anticipated repairs and updates, we approached the bank for a loan.

After carefully investigating foundation repair companies, we chose one offering a lifetime transferable warranty. Sounded like a safe bet, or so we thought.

The company installed additional piers and leveled the house. Confident in the repairs, we optimistically proceeded with the updates. Removing the dated wall paper, replastering and repainting, replacing the floors with new wood laminate provided a fresh new look. Satisfied with the work, we paid the contractors and expected to be done with the problem.

Within six months, the cracks reappeared. Disheartened, but grateful for a lifetime warranty, we contacted the foundation repair company. They came back and adjusted the piers. Hopeful, we expected the problem to be solved.

This time, a little less trusting, we weren't so quick to repair and repaint. "Let's wait a few months and see what happens."

Good call. The problem persisted.

After multiple attempts to adjust the piers without lasting results, the workers ultimately poured concrete in the center of the house. This time it seemed to provide a long-term, if not permanent, solution.

Weary of replastering, my crafty husband decided to create an accent wall in the bedroom with cedar fence boards. He placed them at a diagonal slant, creating an aesthetic that pleased us both. No longer naïve, we anticipated the foundation problems to plague us.

We fully expected to live into our retirement years in

this home. However, circumstances changed and life happened. We purchased property in a rural community and made plans for retirement. Sooner rather than later, we sold our suburban home and began work on our new one in the country. We transferred the foundation problem along with the life-time warranty to the buyer.

My husband micromanaged the entire building process of our new home. Determined to do all he could to prevent foundation issues, he insisted on extra piers drilled to bedrock to support the foundation.

Before the walls went up, we spent a weekend writing scripture on the studs and on the foundation of the structure. As an act of worship, we dedicated ourselves and our home to serve and glorify God. On the foundation, we chose a reference from Matthew.

Therefore, everyone who hears these words of mine and puts them into practice is like a wise man who built his house on the rock. The rain came down, the streams rose, and the winds blew and beat against that house; yet it did not fall, because it had its foundation on the rock. But everyone who hears these words of mine and does not put them into practice is like a foolish man who built his house on sand. The rain came down, the streams rose, and the winds blew and beat against that house, and it fell with a great crash. (Matthew 7:24-27 NIV).

We grew to love our little community and lived contentedly with a few close neighbors. As the development grew, houses sprung up all around us. A young couple purchased the property directly across the street. We welcomed them to the neighborhood and listened to them describe plans to build their dream home. They rented a house in town and came to the building site regularly. We observed as they worked diligently to clear the land and experts poured the foundation. It appeared to be solid and ready to receive the structure that would be their home. The young man erected a shed to house the tools he planned to use in construction.

Progress halted abruptly due to the couple's divorce. He moved into a recreational vehicle on the property. With no progress on the planned build, home owner's regulations forced a move. He vacated, leaving only a concrete slab and the deteriorating eyesore previously used as a tool shed.

The most recent owners, investors with no plans to build, removed the shed and cleaned up the homesite. A foundation waits, an open invitation to finish what started as a sweet dream.

In Jesus' Sermon on the mount, he contrasted stories of two foundations. One built on the rock and the other on the sand. The wise man builds on a rock, while a foolish one builds on the sand, taking no care to ensure solid groundwork. Jesus cautions us to take time and care in establishing a strong base, so we can withstand the storms of life.

A quarter century later, our home stands firm without signs of foundation problems, providing shelter in storms, warmth in winter and cool respite from the brutal summer heat. We welcome friends and family to help us make memories.

Each time, I leave my driveway, I contrast foundations. Our previous home, threatened by a faulty one, may continue to need shoring up. Our current home erected on a firm concrete base, serves a place where we continue to live and enjoy abundant blessings. Across the street, a solid site still awaits a structure, not accomplishing its intended purpose, a sad commentary on an unfulfilled promise.

Jesus admonished his followers. Make sure you build on a solid foundation and count the cost before you begin, so your life will stand firm, serve its intended purpose, and finish strong.

Prayer of an Abundant Heart

Dear Lord,
You are the foundation supporting every detail of life.
Without You, everything crumples.
You have been faithful to sustain me through hard times.
You have protected me through literal storms.
Thank You for our home and for the shelter it provides.
I can rest in the assurance of Your power over every situation.
You are the strength of my life allowing me to stand firm.
I praise and thank You.
I stand in awe of You.

Personal Reflection

_____

_____

_____

_____

_____

_____

_____

_____

_____

_____

_____

_____

_____

_____

Restoring Joy

God's Word

You turned my wailing into dancing; You removed my sackcloth and clothed me with joy, that my heart may sing Your praises and not be silent, LORD, my God, I will praise You forever. (Psalm 30: 11-12 NIV).

Reflection of an Abundant Heart

This is the day that the Lord has made. I will rejoice and be glad in it.

This *is the day that the Lord has made. I will rejoice and be glad in it.*

*This **is** the day that the Lord has made. I will rejoice and be glad in it.*

*This is the day that the Lord has made. I will **rejoice** and* ***be glad*** *in it.*

*This is the day that the Lord has made. I **will** rejoice and be glad in it.*

This is the day that the Lord has made. ***I WILL REJOICE and BE GLAD*** *in it. (Psalm 118:24 KJV).*

On especially dark days, the woman found herself singing as she went about her daily chores. She wasn't happy. In fact, she struggled with dismal circumstances in a very difficult relationship. She determined not to allow situations to steal her joy and chose joy over despair.

Some days she repeatedly sang the familiar chorus or

repeated the verse from the Psalms through tears adding emphasis appropriate to the day's circumstance. Other days she fought despair, sought Holy Spirit's guidance for a reason to rejoice. Her situation remained difficult, yet she chose joy.

Been there? If we are honest, we all have. Not every day is filled with an enthusiastic cheerleader type of happiness. Life on earth produces saddening events.

Very real situations threaten to steal our joy. We weep over injustice and sorrow for those who suffer. Sin broke our world and until God eternally restores it, there will be suffering and distress

While both joy and happiness are positive emotions, they differ dramatically. Joy endures and generates from within, while external events trigger happiness. A particular moment bringing excitement or exhilaration sparks happiness. Joy differs as an abiding state of being contented with life.

Can we choose joy, when we can't find reasons to be happy in the midst of miserable situations?

The answer is a resounding, of course, we can.

The Psalmist understood life without joy. He implored the Lord.

Restore to me the joy of your salvation and grant me a willing spirit, to sustain me. (Psalm 51:12 NIV).

God restored David. He can and will do the same for you and me.

If you feel joyless, don't stay that way.

Be honest with your Father. Ask God to restore your joy. Scripture reminds us, *you have not because you do not ask God. (James 4:2 NIV).*

Jesus came to offer us an abundant life. His perfect plan is to restore what the enemy stole.

The thief comes only to steal and kill and destroy; I have come

that they may have life, and have it to the full. (John 10:10 NIV).

Reflect on the joy of eternal things. God's great love for you, salvation, forgiven sins, and Holy Spirit's presence giving you power, comfort, and strength.

Rejoice in the blessings of each new day.

Because of the LORD's great love we are not consumed, for his compassions never fail. They are new every morning; great is your faithfulness. (Lamentations 3:22-23 NIV).

Winnie the Pooh extolls the wisdom of focusing on the present.

Today is my favorite day. Yesterday, when it was tomorrow, it was too much day for me. A. A. Milne

Sing and cry out to the Lord from your heart. Like my friend, find a song to express your determination to rejoice in each day. Let music express your emotions. Praise and worship God with a grateful heart. As you express gratitude, the more reasons you will find to thank and praise Him.

Surround yourself with believers who hold you accountable and ignite joy in each other.

Always remember how much God loves you. Think often and be encouraged by the hope of eternal life in heaven.

For God so loved the world that he gave his one and only Son, that whoever believes in him shall not perish but have eternal life. (John 3: 16 NIV).

Live fully! Celebrate! Rejoice!

Prayer of an Abundant Heart

Lord, I confess.
Too often, my heart is heavy.
The burdens of day-to-day life on earth weigh heavy.
I get bogged down in the sorrow of a broken world.
I lift my head and heart to You, the source of my joy.
Draw me close.
Like the psalmist, I implore,
RESTORE MY JOY.
Remind me of the many things sparking joy in my life.
I have a breath in my lungs.
I have purpose.
I am loved.
You promise me a future, here and now and for eternity.
Keep me focused on my blessings and Your faithfulness.
I WILL PRAISE and REJOICE.

Personal Reflection

_____

_____

_____

_____

_____

_____

_____

_____

_____

_____

_____

Tell the Old Stories

God's Word:

Because of the Lord's great love we are not consumed, for his compassions never fail. They are new every morning; great is your faithfulness. (Lamentations 3:22-23 NIV).

Refection of an Abundant Heart

As I sat down at the dinner table, my phone rang. The caller identified herself as the mammographer from the local clinic. "The doctor reviewed your films. You need to return for additional views and a breast sonogram. Under-standing the anxiety this call causes, I want to get you in before the weekend. I have an appointment tomorrow morning at 9:30. Can you come at that time?"

I responded without hesitation, "Thank you for getting me in promptly. I'll be there,"

Disconnecting the call, I returned to my dinner and for the moment silenced my racing thoughts. Throughout the rest of the evening, the what ifs and what next threatened the peace I struggled to maintain. Thirteen years separated the current challenge from my initial diagnosis. Yet, I vividly recalled every detail of the first call.

"I'm 99.9% sure this is nothing, but we need to evaluate an area of concern near your chest wall to be absolutely sure." The radiologist offered assurance in an attempt to quell my escalating fears.

Statistics mean nothing when facing your own crisis.

All the 99.9% negative results counted for nothing, when mine was the .01% positive. It was 100% for me.

Memories of the initial diagnostic imaging, additional tests, surgery and treatment surfaced. Knowledge might be powerful but can also be a curse. Because I knew too much, discarding my oncology nurse hat proved impossible. A recurrence would not mean a simple lumpectomy followed by radiation. It would be far more involved and invasive. Whether I wanted to admit it, and while I maintained an active, healthy lifestyle, thirteen years of survival added the same number of years to my age and risk. A cascade of menacing recollections and unbidden thoughts robbed me of sleep. My rational brain finally kicked in, and admonished my conscious mind, *staying awake all night will not change a thing.*

I prayed "Lord, you understand my anxiety. I'm helpless to change this situation. I know you've got this, so I'm letting you take it. Please let me get the rest I need to face tomorrow."

While this response sounds simplistic, I did not arrive here without a great deal of trial and error. Like other firstborn children, my desire to maintain control drove efforts to solve everything for everyone around me. Failed attempts served as proof of my inability to control anything. A quote from an unknown source indicted me. "When you try to control everything, you enjoy nothing."

Thoughts of anxious days and sleepless nights in my past reminded me, *there is peace when I let go and surrender the illusion of control.*

Days earlier, a friend shared a webcast link. Totally unrelated to health issues, the speaker encouraged listeners to "tell the old stories, examples of faith and reminders of how God worked in the past."

As I drove to the clinic, I applied this principle. *Remember your own stories.* God flooded my conscious mind with memories of His faithful presence throughout my life—all the many times He carried me through tough times

During times of financial difficulties, layoffs, and economic downturns, God provided a way. We never lacked food or shelter.

Over our more than fifty-year marriage, my husband suffered multiple life-threatening illnesses, injuries and mishaps, some involving ladders and his own lack of good judgement. Yet, he recovered and continues to pursue most of the things he enjoys.

However, nothing prepared me for the toughest year of my life. My ten-year old daughter's malignant brain tumor altered our entire existence. A year of diagnosis and treatment followed by associated and significant long-term and late effects changed my perspective on everything. We prayed for a miracle, and over four decades of cancer free survival evidenced God's miraculous power. He proved faithful in the most difficult of circumstances. My unchallenged faith grew exponentially during my daughter's illness. I learned to rely God for provision, wisdom and hope. I observed the cultivation of faith in the lives of the many people our story touched.

God sustained me, as I walked through one crisis after another. Though I desired to avoid the crucible of suffering, each trial caused me to rely more fully on Him. The hardest experiences shaped the person I am.

My own cancer journey paled in comparison to the threat posed to my daughter. Compared to previous experiences, today represented a small bump in the road of life.

I slept through an early alarm and hurriedly got dressed. I thanked God for the mammographer's sensitivity, who empathized with the inevitable angst accompanying call-backs for cancer survivors.

Arriving at the clinic, I texted a few prayer warriors assuring them and myself, no matter the results of this pending test, with God's help, I would make it through this.

I checked in and struggled to maintain a sense of peace. My mind raced ahead. *Which oncologist would I use? What surgeon?*

STOP!

Take this one minute, one step at a time.

The proficient mammographer performed the necessary exams. The radiologist entered the room and with her first words relieved all anxiety. "I think you are fine. I just want to look and make absolutely sure. The mammogram didn't clearly show the area behind your original scar. After additional test and review, I am confident in saying there is no area of concern."

In a heartbeat, my mood changed from mildly apprehensive to absolutely elated. "Thank you. Thank you. Thank you. I didn't think I was anxious, but now I'm really relieved and peaceful."

Driving away, I celebrated being a thirteen-year cancer survivor. I briefly wondered; *Would I feel so elated if I faced recurrence?*

I would never stand in line to sign up for the next crisis. However, I am secure in the knowledge that God faithfully walks with me through life, every challenge, and in every joy.

In the midst of disappointment, illness, political chaos, pandemic, whatever my circumstance, God is in control. He is always with me, sustaining me and giving me peace.

While I never say I am grateful for cancer, I do express gratitude for lessons learned through the cancer experience. Perhaps the greatest of those lessons—**Life is a gift.** On the day my daughter arrived, I acknowledged her life as a precious gift. The cancer experience, hers as well as my own, heightened my appreciation for our lives. I recognized the fragility of life. On the hardest days, my gratitude consisted of the ability to simply put one foot in front of the other, as I continued to look for more reasons to be thankful.

When I express gratitude for the gift of life, the awareness of my many other blessings intensifies. Each sunrise represents another opportunity to live fully.

I choose to embrace life with an attitude of gratitude. If I ever need a reason to celebrate, I recall and share the old stories.

Prayer of an Abundant Heart

Precious Lord,
I celebrate the new day.
Forgive me when I take this gift of life for granted.
When the struggles of daily living threaten to overwhelm, remind me of all You've seen me through.
When I stress over minor inconveniences and trivial circumstances, help me regain perspective.
Give me opportunities to share the stories of your faithfulness and encourage others on this journey of life.
You are always faithful and I am abundantly grateful.

Personal Reflection

_____

_____

_____

_____

_____

_____

_____

_____

_____

_____

_____

_____

_____

_____

_____

_____

_____

_____

_____

_____

_____

_____

_____

_____

_____

Replenishing Hope

God's Word

Even youths grow tired and weary, and young men stumble and fall; but those who hope in the LORD will renew their strength. They will soar on wings like eagles; they will run and not grow weary; they will walk and not be faint. (Isaiah 40:30-31 NIV).

Reflection of an Abundant Heart

I intently focused on the dwindling hope candle. It's only the third Sunday. That candle will never make it until Christmas. My thoughts drifted as I contemplated the candle and its meaning – A recurring thought stayed with me, "Where do I go when my hope runs low?"

Because we live in a broken world, our hope will run low. We experience broken relationships, poor health, financial problems – fill in the blank with your own endless list of challenges. Feelings of hopelessness and despair rise to the surface. Like the dwindling candle, our hope runs low and burns out.

Christmas offers hope to a hopeless world. When the prophets despaired, God broke through to a dark world and sent His Son. Zachariah and Elizabeth, Simeon, and Anna all hoped and waited for the Messiah. Though the prophets foretold His coming, God remained silent for hundreds of years. Perhaps they'd given up hope. But God!

God honored their faithfulness, answered their prayers, and allowed them to see Messiah.

A supernatural star, mysterious men from a distant land, unexpected gifts arrived at exactly the right time. A divine dream warned the family and the wisemen of Herod's crazed, evil plan. This story reminds us – God's ways are not our ways, and His plans rarely fit our expectations – or come in any easily comprehended package. God planned for our salvation. He provided for Jesus, Mary, and Joseph. He will do the same for you and for me.

We look at our circumstances through the lens of here and now, while God looks at through the lens of eternity?

So… Where do we go when we need reassurance and confidence in God's plan and provision? How do we deal with uncertainty while we wait for the deferred hope we've been promised?

John the Baptist faced the same problem. As he sat in Herod's jail, his hope surely ran low. From his perspective, he'd done everything he was called to do. Yet, he found himself in a prison awaiting execution. Perhaps he questioned his purpose. Perhaps he wondered if Jesus was truly the promised Messiah? He sent his followers to ask, *"Are you the one who is to come, or should we expect someone else?" (Matthew 11:3. NIV).*

Jesus responded, not with a direct answer. Rather he pointed John to the prophesies in Isaiah. Go and report to John what you hear and see: *"The blind receive their sight, the lame walk, those with leprosy are cleansed, the deaf hear, the dead are raised and the poor are told the good news." (Matthew 11:4-5 NIV).*

Jesus' words reassured John. As an avid student of scripture, John surely made the connection. Jesus was exactly who He claimed to be and would fulfill His promises. John still faced difficult circumstances, but God's word provided everything he needed to keep going and finish his own mission.

As we wait for God's promises to be fulfilled in our

lives, we can rely on the Scriptures to deal with times when our hope runs low.

Unlike the candle which cannot regenerate, our source of hope knows no limits. Scripture repeatedly reminds us of God's plan for our lives and of His promises to sustain and be Emmanuel, God with us, while we wait for our eternal hope.

The final chapters of the New Testament assure us there is indeed something better to come and we can trust God's plan for us.

I saw the Holy City, the new Jerusalem, coming down out of heaven from God, prepared as a bride beautifully dressed for her husband. And I heard a loud voice from the throne saying,

"Look! God's dwelling place is now among the people, and he will dwell with them. They will be his people, and God himself will be with them and be their God. He will wipe every tear from their eyes. There will be no more death or mourning or crying or pain, for the old order of things has passed away." He who was seated on the throne said, "I am making everything new!" Then he said, "Write this down, for these words are trustworthy and true." (Revelations 21:2-5 NIV).

Unwrap the gift of hope.

Celebrate our perpetual source.

Prayer of an Abundant Heart

Precious Savior and Lord,
When things seem hopeless, You make a way.
You remind me to trust your plan for my future, now and into eternity.
I have reason to celebrate.
You prove faithful to sustain me and be with me through all life's challenges.
My hope is in you, Lord.
I trust you to work all things for my good.
Help me remain faithful, while I wait for your perfect will.

Personal Reflection

_____

_____

_____

_____

_____

_____

_____

_____

_____

_____

_____

_____

_____

_____

_____

_____

_____

_____

_____

_____

_____

_____

_____

_____

_____

A View from the Top

God's Word

Brothers, I do not consider myself yet to have taken hold of it. But one thing I do; forgetting what is behind and straining toward what is ahead, I press on toward the goal to win the prize for which God has called me heavenward in Christ Jesus. (Philippians 3:13-14 NIV).

Reflection of an Abundant Heart

I prayed as I merged onto Interstate 20, eastbound, perfectly on schedule, "What do you want to teach me, today, Father?"

My eyes scanned the horizon for any hint of storm clouds. Nothing threatened to disturb the atmosphere. The bright blue sky held the promise of a beautiful new day.

Grateful for an early morning commute free of traffic jams, which allowed a preoccupation with family demands. I searched the sky for insight from God. Daddy's cancer struggle lurked foremost in my mind.

Diagnosed with stage IV lung cancer, my father fought valiantly and amazed everyone. He repeatedly stated, "When God is ready for me to go, I will go. I am ready when he is ready for me."

For almost three years he endured multiple chemotherapy regimens and responded positively to each one. He continued to live every day to his fullest capacity. When the last regimen failed to arrest the growth, the doctor delivered dreaded news. He advised no further treatment. All options exhausted, the physician recommended hospice.

A new team now managed Dad's daily care. Over a matter of a few weeks, his health rapidly deteriorated. I prayed for pain relief and an end to his prolonged suffering.

I thought about Dad's acknowledgment of God's sovereignty and chuckled. "The interior decorators must be putting the finishing touches on the mansion, perfecting things for the move-in date."

As I pondered thoughts of a heavenly home, a streak of white clouds appeared in the previously clear sky. The line stretched across my vision. It moved upward without interruption rising endlessly into the heavens. I imagined Daddy pushing forward uphill, climbing a road that led to heaven and an encounter with God.

In contrast to this visual image, my spiritual life failed to show steady progress. Far too often my journey mingled with ups and downs, with many highs and lows. Through the years, I moved close to God, then slipped backwards or slid downhill. I questioned, doubted, and fell short of my earthly goals.

My thoughts turn to the long incline near my home. My lack of physical exercise and poor stamina causes me to struggle with the steep uphill climb. I attempt such a feat with great difficulty.

Is the climb worth it? Most definitely! The hills and valleys playing against the sunset create a magnificent landscape. Because I know what waits for me at the top of the hill, I press forward to experience it again and again.

Though scripture describes the grandeur of heaven, my spiritual eyes can only imagine the glories awaiting me. Hope encourages me to keep moving forward and upward to realize God's promise.

He speaks to my heart, "Stay faithful. Keep climbing. I promise the view is worth the effort."

My Daddy no longer imagines heaven. He now experiences the reality for eternity. I can almost hear his slow Texas drawl, "Keep walking. Press on. It is beautiful here! Come on in. I want to show you the view!"

Prayer of an Abundant Heart

Dear Father,

I long for all those I love who are with You in heaven.

I wonder if they can feel how much I love and miss them.

I rejoice in the knowledge they no longer experience pain, suffering, or death.

They enjoy life without earthly limitations.

Give me the strength to continue living every day as if it might be my last on earth.

Forgive me when I miss the opportunity to celebrate the life You grant me with each new day.

Give me the grace and courage to be all that You designed me to be.

Personal reflection

_____

_____

_____

_____

_____

_____

_____

_____

_____

_____

_____

Wishing on a Star

God's Word
Now faith is the substance of things hoped for, the evidence of things not seen. (Hebrews 11:1 KJV).

Reflection of an Abundant Heart
> *Star Light, Star Bright,*
> *First star I see tonight,*
> *Wish I may, Wish I might,*
> *Have the wish I wish tonight.*
> *Traditional English Nursery Rhyme—*
> *published 19th Century*

Literature and music ascribe a certain mystical, magical quality to the night sky. The first star appears each night capturing the attention of poets and songwriters. The sun sets and before the moon makes its nightly arrival, the evening star rises in the western sky. However, what we refer to as the evening star isn't a star at all. It's the planet Venus. Whoa! Very disappointing, since poetry and music emphasize the importance of wishing on the first star of the evening. Call me naïve but wishing on a star seems so much more romantic, though others might argue that Venus possesses a romantic history of her own.

Little girls dream of the fairy tale life she envisions for her future. Maybe some of those fairy tales come true, but that is certainly not true for most of us. Reality disappoints. Life is hard. Things rarely work out exactly as planned.

In our best moments, we acknowledge, "God knows what is best for me. He sees the whole picture. I trust His plan."

Since we live and work on an earthly timetable with physical limitations, acknowledging God's plan can be difficult. I often find myself pleading for Him to give me a little glimpse of His plan and will for me.

What is a wish, anyway? How does it differ from hopes and dreams. The dictionary defines a wish as something longed for, wanted, or desired. Our dreams include fond hopes and aspirations. Hope is characterized by an expectation that the thing hoped for will happen. Hope involves not only the desire, but an expectation that the desire will be fulfilled.

While we might wish for a new pair of earrings or dream of the perfect event, we hope that medication will restore us to health.

Though dreams inspire us to set goals and make things happen, those wishes are fluid, constantly changing. Life alters our priorities. What we yearn for in our youth often differs from the desires of maturity. Hope encourages us to keep on striving to reach our goals.

When the world says, 'Give up,' hope whispers, 'Try it one more time. Anonymous

Hope provides our greatest resource for facing the realities of life. In prayer, we earnestly rely on God for the courage to face uncertainties of life and ask him to supply the strength needed for every challenge.

Prayer of an Abundant Heart
Father God, Sustainer of the Universe,
Thank You for the evening star, or planet Venus, as a reminder of
Your constant presence in my life.
Thank You for allowing me to bring my wishes and dreams to You.
Forgive me when I bring a laundry list of wants and needs. Help me to
be grateful in all circumstances.
Above all, I thank You for the assurance, You are the hope for my
future; today, tomorrow, and eternally.

Personal Reflection

_____

_____

_____

_____

_____

_____

_____

_____

_____

_____

_____

_____

_____

_____

_____

Lost in the Moment

God's Word

The heavens declare the glory of God; the skies proclaim the work of his hands. (Psalm 19: 1 NIV).

Reflection of an Abundant Heart

A massive, red-orange ball blazed, totally filling the early evening sky.

The full moon appeared low on the horizon, so close it seemed possible to reach out and touch it. Nothing along the country road—no clouds—no stars—nothing in the landscape competed for my attention.

I paused, fully absorbed in the moment.

Awe-inspiring! Astounding! Astonishing!

Beautiful! Breath-taking! Brilliant!

Dazzling!

Extravagant! Exquisite!

Marvelous! Magnificent!

Splendid! Stunning! Spectacular!

My mind searched unsuccessfully for adjectives to describe the scene and capture the emotions evoked by the experience.

Celebrating the Father, I offered praise for the His creation.

As my drive brought the city into view, it became more difficult to focus on the moon and surrounding sky. Too many distractions clamored for my attention. Busy traffic with vehicles rushed by me. Buildings blocked my vision. Obstructions and activity diverted my focus from the Creator's art show.

As the moon rose higher in the sky, the stars as well as artificial lights of the city competed with the moon.

The Creator's masterpiece, so captivating a few moments earlier, existed only in my memory.

But what a memory!

Overwhelmed with gratitude for this divine appointment, this single moment in time, I indulged in a moment to bask in His presence. Being still and knowing that He is God. He will be exalted in the heavens and on earth.

Prayer of an Abundant Heart

Awesome Creator,
I praise You for the gift of creation.
Thank You for allowing me to witness Your handiwork.
Help me to always look for the magnificent in the midst of the commonplace and never be too busy to stop and appreciate creation.
I praise you for the work You are completing in me.

Personal Reflection

_____

_____

_____

_____

_____

_____

_____

_____

No Problem * Don't Worry * Be Happy

God's Word

Give your entire attention to what God is doing right now, and don't get worked up about what may or may not happen tomorrow. God will help you deal with whatever hard things come up when the time comes. (Matthew 5:34 The Message).

Reflections of an Abundant Heart

Despite the forecast for a clear, sunny day without indication of storms, ominous clouds appeared in the early morning sky. A threatening, angry atmosphere demanded attention. Though everything in my experience assured me these clouds presented no storm danger, some vague forewarning triggered an unreasonable fear.

Within a matter of seconds, the sky cleared. Threat averted. Tension relieved. Serenity restored. Bright sunshine required shades for clear vision.

Like the threatening sky, anxiety evokes a response of dread. Many things in our world cause apprehension. When things threaten our protected, insulated world, we seek a sense of calm and security. Quite frequently, those concerns causing the most anxiety and worry never happen. The tragedies which shake our existence often occur like a sudden storm, without warning—events we never consider possible and calamities we never anticipate with no power to prevent.

Scripture admonishes us not to worry about

tomorrow.

Has anyone by fussing before the mirror ever gotten taller by so much as an inch? If fussing can't even do that, why fuss at all? Walk into the fields and look at the wildflowers. They don't fuss with their appearance—but have you ever seen color and design quite like it? The ten best-dressed men and women in the country look shabby alongside them. If God gives such attention to the wildflowers, most of them never even seen, don't you think he'll attend to you, take pride in you, do his best for you? (Luke 12: 28-28 The Message).

Like the clouds that gather, threatening but never causing a storm, often anxieties linger and never escalate to a crisis. Before we formulate a solution to the problem, the circumstance resolves. Even those situations with no resolution look different in the bright light of a new day.

Give God your anxieties. He desires for us to live each day to the fullest, trusting in His care, and seizing opportunities to reflect His glory.

Prayer of an Abundant Heart

All Mighty Father,
Thank you for the assurance of your consistent control.
You are big enough to handle any problem.
Focus my attention on the sunshine and not on the clouds.
Keep me strong in the knowledge that You will stand with me whatever situation I face.
Don't let the anxieties in my life weaken my witness for You.

Personal Reflection

_____

_____

_____

_____

_____

_____

_____

_____

_____

_____

_____

_____

_____

_____

_____

_____

_____

_____

_____

_____

_____

_____

_____

_____

_____

Pruning for Beauty and Fruitfulness

God's Word

He cuts off every branch in me that bears no fruit, while every branch that does bear fruit, he prunes so that it will be even more fruitful. You are already clean because of the word I have spoken to you. (John 15:2-3 NIV).

Reflection of an Abundant Heart

Each February, the knockout roses in my yard undergo severe lopping. Master gardeners recommend a reduction of at least one-third of each bushes' size. One plant in the front flower bed grows so prolifically, I cut it cut back to ground level each year. If it fails to rebound, I propose a less invasive replacement. A daunting task requires a full day of manual labor, cutting and either bundling for trash pick-up or stacking in a pile to wait for a common-sense time to burn brush.

Why do gardeners prune not only roses but other flowering plants?

Pruning benefits trees and shrubs in numerous ways. The removal of dead, diseased or damaged branches promotes health, encourages growth, and enhances the beauty of the plants. Improved airflow and penetration of sunlight make plants more resilient to pests and disease. Eliminating weaker, damaged branches allows energy to focus on healthy growth. Shaping and training controls size and optimizes fruit or flower production.

As warmer weather signals the arrival of spring, new

growth emerges. By mid-April, blossoms cover the bushes in a colorful display of buds and flowers.

Throughout the season removal of the spent flowers encourages new flower production and a health appearance. Landscapers refer to this process as deadheading. Diligent attention to this task produces a recuring burst of new buds, rewarding the gardener with an extended season of beautiful flowers.

The gospel of John records an analogy of pruning to encourage the believer to be fruitful. He lops off every non-fruit bearing branch from our lives, so we will produce more fruit.

As God removes obstacles to my spiritual growth, He shapes my life for fruitfulness. Eliminating these hindrances, allows me to focus on my relationship with Him. Light exposes unconfessed sin and leads to a deeper desire for holiness. Pain and difficult circumstances may cause me to examine my life, seek divine guidance, and expose areas of my heart in need of strategic intervention.

Though painful, I submit to the ongoing essential process. The ultimate goal produces more fruit for God's glory as I become more mature and better equipped to serve Him.

Prayer of an Abundant Heart
Creator God, Master Gardener,
Thank you for the beauty of your creation and lessons from nature.
As I observe the benefits of pruning the plants in my yard, reveal the areas of lifelessness in me.
Remind me to willing submit the dead places for removal.
Make me willing to eliminate any hinderances to my relationship with You.
As I see the flowers emerge, show me where my life can glorify and serve you.
I desire to be fruitful.

Personal Reflection

Quench the Thirst

God's Word

For I will pour water on the thirsty land, and streams on the dry ground; I will pour out my Spirit on your offspring, and my blessing on your descendants. Isaiah 44:3 NIV

Reflection of an Abundant Heart

As I enter my small rural community, a sign greets me. "Burn Ban—Fire Danger." I search for any sign of green but see only dry, dead plants and grasses. The lack of any form of moisture causes the ground to crack and separate. The land suffers from draught.

Plants, animals, and humans—all living things require water for survival. If the human body becomes dehydrated, the entire system gets out of control. The ability to sustain life is threatened.

Drinking water easily corrects thirst in a healthy individual. Simply turn on the faucet and drink a glass of water to quench physical thirst. Correcting spiritual dryness proves more challenging. When our souls thirst, only God can satisfy that need.

Sometimes life's circumstances wring out every last drop of moisture. My soul cries for nourishment. Weary and arid, crisis upon crisis zaps my energy and strength.

Wouldn't it be great to have a "spiritual faucet" that could be turned on whenever you need a drink of Holy Spirit? To discover a magic formula for renewal of divine strength?

God does have a word on this subject!

Whoever drinks the water I give them will never thirst. Indeed, the water I give them will become in them a spring of water welling up to eternal life. (John 4:14 NIV).

Christ asks only that I accept His gift—the gift of living water.

Prayer of an Abundant Heart

Dear God, my provider, my sustainer, my nourishment,
I thirst for you.
The world drains moisture from my spirit.
Don't let me dry up and wither away.
I desire to know you more fully, to flourish and bloom.
Reveal every barrier that keeps me from experiencing Your fountain,
Keep my reservoir full. I open my heart to receive the water only You can supply.

Personal Reflection

_____

_____

_____

_____

_____

_____

_____

_____

_____

_____

_____

The Voice of Experience

God's Word

Encourage one another daily, as long as it is called today, so that none of you may be hardened by sin's deceitfulness. (Hebrews 3:13 NIV).

Reflection of an Abundant Heart

An ordinary morning commute presented nothing unusual. Earlier in the week, storms and dark clouds threatened, but not on this day. Warmer temperatures, promised an early spring. Leaving home on time insured a relatively stress-free drive to work. Music filled the vehicle, and I sang along with worship music as I drove the familiar highway. As I topped the hill, brake lights caught my attention, and traffic came to a standstill. A long line of cars waited for an opening to move forward.

A familiar occurrence on city freeways, such incidences rarely happened on my drive through the country. Highway patrol officers diverted traffic from the state highway onto a farm to market road, which indicated a serious accident likely involving a fatality. I prayed for the accident victims and for the families who would soon receive unthinkable news.

Unfamiliar with the back roads, I hesitated. Briefly I considered a U-turn to the small town on the main highway to get directions for an alternate route. Instead, I blindly followed the cars in front of me assuming they knew the way. Unfortunately, the entire line of cars followed as aimlessly as a sheep without a shepherd. I expected to cross a road reconnecting me to the highway beyond the scene of the accident. Indeed, it did lead me back to the highway. I drove for over a half hour in a huge circle which took me back to town, which I would have reached in less than ten minutes had I taken the U-turn option.

I located the spot where locals met daily, a charming feature of living in the country. I made my way through the convenience store and back to the grill, where I found a group of men enjoying coffee, breakfast, and conversation. I approached their table and asked directions for an alternate route. They happily redirected me. Though news of the accident reached the group, they didn't know the exact location of the wreck. One farmer suggested the route I just traveled. Been there, done that. Nope, that wouldn't work. Another gentleman offered clear instructions, complete with landmarks, and soon I resumed my commute with an appropriate course correction.

I followed his instructions. Because of the distance to the cut off, I questioned whether I clearly understood the directions. Just as I was about to give up and turn around, the Y in the road appeared and signs confirmed the route. I saw familiar sights assuring me of the right path.

I made some poor choices in my attempt to redirect my route. Incorrectly assuming they knew the way, I chose to follow the wrong person. Ultimately, I made the right choice and sought out someone who possessed the knowledge and experience to offer wise counsel.

Life situations often leave us feeling lost, wandering in continuous loops. Sometimes we foolishly choose to blindly follow someone who is equally lost. When we act wisely, we seek out someone with the knowledge and experience to redirect a struggling traveler.

How much effort is wasted trying to find the right

direction, moving aimlessly in circles while accomplishing nothing?

Expending the energy and effort to seek out wise counsel proves definitely worth the effort.

Prayer of an Abundant Heart

Loving Lord,

Help me to maintain proper perspective.

A traffic detour represents a minor inconvenience, when I consider the pain and grief of unexpectedly and tragically losing a loved one.

Comfort those who receive tragic news. Hold them close and bless them with sweet memories.

Place in my life mentors who possess experience, knowledge, and wisdom to help me through difficult circumstances.

Make me aware of opportunities to be an encourager to fellow travelers who struggle to find the way.

Thank you for trusting me enough to bring me through the fire of adversity so that I can help others through their time of testing.

Personal Reflection

_____

_____

_____

_____

_____

_____

_____

_____

_____

_____

_____

Altered Perception

God's Word
Cleanse me with hyssop, and I will be clean; wash me, and I will be whiter than snow. (Psalm 51: 7 NIV)

Reflection of an Abundant Heart
As I pull onto the highway, I can barely see the road ahead. The dirt on my filthy windshield obscures my vision. Dust and spattered bugs from last evening's commute cover the glass. I press the button to release windshield washing fluid only to find an empty reservoir. The wipers continue to swipe across the window and only serve to smear the dirt and cover the surface. I adjust my position looking for a clear spot to allow me a view of the road ahead. Though I can see through the dirt, my altered perspective hampers my driving ability.

Several miles into my morning commute, I stop at a service station, locate the cleaning wand, and remove at least enough of the muck to allow an unobstructed view and safe passage on the highway. To really do the job right I need a car wash with heavy-duty machines.

Like the dirt on my windshield, sin separates me from God, creates barriers, and obscures my spiritual vision. It clouds my perspective and changes my view of God's plan for my life. As hard as I try to clean up my own act, I cannot be perfect. In my own strength, I'm unable to change even for one day. I can never be good enough or pure enough.

Fortunately, God made a better way.

Christ came and died not only to give me salvation but to show me how to live. His sacrifice cleanses me from the inside out. I no longer need to follow the ritualistic cleansing with hyssop. The sweet smelling, bitter tasting mint only works temporarily.

With my heart transformed, my vision of God's plan for my life clears. No more pushing the button, and finding the reservoir dry. The endless supply of God's cleansing water always remains full.

Prayer of an Abundant Heart

Lord,
Make my heart clean before you, so that I can see clearly the plan you have for me.
Cleanse me so You can use me to do and be all You have for me to do an be.

Personal Reflection

_____

_____

_____

_____

_____

_____

_____

_____

_____

_____

_____

_____

The Colors of Spring

God's Word

Consider how the lilies grow. They do not labor or spin.

Yet I tell you, not even Solomon in all his splendor was dressed like one of these. It that is how God clothes the grass of the field, which is here today and tomorrow is thrown into the fire, how much more will he clothe you, O you of little faith. (Luke 12:27-28 KJV).

Reflection of an Abundant Heart

I love spring mornings. The sound of birds chirping and light streaming through my window invites me to join the reawakening of the day. In contrast to dark winter mornings, bright sun lights the world as I begin my commute to the city.

Spring celebrates every shade on the color wheel. Blue, yellow, and red wildflowers accent fields of green grass. The sun shines with tints of orange and yellow against the background of a brilliant blue sky. Purple irises in cultivated beds complete the wheel of primary and secondary colors. Blending and mixing the colors create a dramatic landscape with intense hues.

Blankets of bluebonnets bank long stretches along the highways and serve as the celebrated superstars of the season. Each spring, Texans eagerly anticipate this show of color and make plans to visit the bluebonnet trails. We gaze at the fields, take pictures, and boast of the beauty of our country side. We act as if we could somehow take credit for any part of this magnificent display.

Unfortunately, nature limits this exhibit—the proliferation of flowers lasts only a brief time. We enjoy the presentation for about three weeks each spring. Delaying the country drive for a week or two can mean you miss the beauty altogether and must wait another year to witness the pride of Texas, our state flower.

If the spring wildflower season stretched into summer and fall, I might be tempted to take the beauty for granted. Being aware of limited blooming time causes me to focus on enjoying them today. Tomorrow may be too late.

Our hectic schedules encourage a natural tendency to take things for granted. We assume tomorrow affords the opportunity to do the things we fail to do today. Tomorrow I'll spend time with my spouse, children, grandchildren, family, or friends.

Unfortunately, tomorrow becomes today. Too often, those opportunities get pushed to the next day and tomorrow never comes. Unless we set priorities, the plans get lost in the busy, harried pace of our lives. We miss little opportunities.

Often, I miss the sweet moments of life because some problem, real or perceived consumes my thoughts and energy. I delay enjoying simple pleasures with my family, because I busy myself with less important things.

Perhaps the most valuable lesson my years as an oncology nurse taught me—life is short.

Many cancer patients articulate one blessing of their diagnosis. Cancer provides an opportunity for significant connections. Unlike death as a result of a fatal heart attack or sudden accident which denies a chance for important conversations, a life limiting diagnosis carries with it the realization, time can longer be taken for granted.

Enjoy the world and everything in it. Mend relationships. Express love. Celebrate life. Like the song says, "Live Like You Were Dying." (Song written by Craig Wiseman and Tim Nichols and recorded by Tim McGraw.)

Like spring flowers, the blooming time of our lives is limited. Time is precious. If we want to build a legacy of love, contentment, and joy, we should start now.

Note: For inspiration, consider listening to "Live Like You Were Dying" recorded by Tim McGraw, and/or "Til You Can't" recorded by Cody Johnson.

Prayer of an Abundant Heart
Dear Father, God
Help me to be content with all the blessing You have given me.
I want to enjoy each moment of life you allow me to live.
Heighten my awareness of the beauty of the world around me.
Give me opportunities to make memories with the ones I love.
Make my legacy be one of contentment, joy and love.

Personal Reflection

Grazing in Unexpected Places

God's Word

Oh, Lord, You have searched me and You know me.
You know when I sit and when I rise,
You perceive my thoughts from afar.
You discern my going out and my lying down;
You are familiar with all my ways.
Before a word is on my tongue
You know it completely, O Lord.
You hem me in, behind and before,
You have laid Your hand upon me.
Such knowledge is too wonderful for me,
too lofty for me to attain.
Where can I go from Your Spirit?
Where can I flee from Your presence?
If I go up to the heavens, You are there.
If I make my bed in the depths, You are there.
If I rise on the wings of the dawn,
if I settle on the far side of the sea,
even there Your hand will guide me;
Your right hand will hold me fast.
(Psalm 139: 1-10 NIV).

Reflection of an Abundant Heart

Captivated by the banks of bluebonnets along the busy thoroughfare, I drove the familiar route on a pleasant spring morning. An unfamiliar scene captured my attention. I shifted my focus to a meadow of green bordered by a large church, parking lots, and a beautiful chapel which serves as the centerpiece of Dallas Baptist University.

The meadow appeared out of place surrounded by so much concrete. The clearly visible skyline of the city emphasized the metropolitan location. This setting seemed the least likely site for a herd of cows. But there they grazed, blissfully unaware of the irony.

Frequently I observe cattle along farm-to-market roads in countryside farms. Surrounded by barns and farmhouses, they feast peacefully in one meadow or another.

I pondered. Do this city cows not know they need to be with their country relatives?

How did they get there?

They don't belong here.

God used the moment to teach me. God knows exactly where each cow finds food. The Psalmist says *the cattle on a thousand hills are his. (Psalm 50:10 NIV)*. Nothing in this world escapes His attention or is beyond his care.

Often in this world, like the cows in the city, I find myself feeling out of place. At times I ask myself, "What am I doing in this situation?

In this place?

Does God really know where I am?

Does He feel my distress?

Does He care?

How can He possibly use me where I am?"

As I trust Him, and rely on His promises, I know the answer to all these questions is a resounding *Yes. Yes, He knows. Yes, He cares. Yes, he will provide for me no matter where I find myself.*

He definitely can and will use every circumstance for good.

Prayer of an Abundant Heart

Thank you, Lord, for Your promise.
You will never leave me or forsake me.
You know where I am every moment of my life and will be with me wherever I go.
Like the cattle, make me content anywhere You place me.
You provide for me and strengthen me in all circumstances.
Don't let me waste the painful times in my life.
Keep me willing to use the difficult times in my life to bring glory to You.
Keep me open to encounters with fellow strugglers who need strength borne of the adversities You have seen me through.

Personal Reflection

_____

_____

_____

_____

_____

_____

_____

_____

_____

_____

_____

_____

_____

Living Waters

God's Word

He said to me; "it is done. I am the Alpha and Omega, the Beginning and the end. To him who is thirsty I will give to drink without cost from the spring of living water. (Revelation 21:6. NIV).

Reflection of an Abundant Heart

The steady beat of raindrops on my roof, encourages me to linger a little longer in my bed and listen to nature's music.

The brook gurgles and then becomes a trickling stream.

A burgeoning river roars rapidly within its banks. Later in the year this same river flows lazily through the countryside.

Lakes produce sounds ranging from the simple lapping of small waves against the side of a boat to whitecaps crashing into the fishing docks on the shore.

More powerful breakers crash onto the rocks along the shore of the ocean. Other waves rhythmically break and roll on to the beach and then recede back into the ocean.

Moving water creates all these incredible sounds.

Springs of living water portray an image of energy and excitement. The sound of rushing water conveys power. Bubbling springs conjure thoughts of happy sounds. Water serves as an accompaniment for our praise in heaven.

Springs of living water in Revelation contrast with still waters in Psalm 23. The quiet waters call us to come away from our chaotic stress filled lives. They beckon us to seek restoration of our souls.

The Lord is my shepherd, I lack nothing. He makes me lie down in green pastures, He leads me beside quiet waters, He refreshes my soul. He guides me along the right paths for his name's sake. (Psalm 23:1-3 NIV).

Still water left undisturbed for an extended period of time becomes stagnant and infected with contaminants. Stagnant water assaults the senses. Even clean water placed in a pool or in a container becomes stagnant and dirty when motionless. Standing water rapidly deteriorates to an unhealthy breeding ground for insects and pests which carry diseases. All stagnant water is still water, but not all still water is stagnant.

A lake without turmoil or choppy waves calms and soothes. Still waters refurbish and ready us for the tasks ahead. However, to accomplish our purpose, activity must occur. We need both; quiet renewal and active inspiration.

God intends our live on earth to be full and exciting. The springs of living water empower us to live fully active, productive lives.

Prayer of an Abundant Heart

Dear Lord,
Forgive me when my life becomes a stagnant pool.
Clean out the areas where destructive thoughts and habits have been allowed to grow.
Help me to live daily with an image of a living, active stream flowing through me.
Fill me so that the living water overflows in a life of service to you.

Personal Reflection

Scattered Light

God's Word

You are the light of the world. A town built on a hill cannot be hidden. Neither do people light a lamp and put it under a bowl. Instead, they put it on its stand, and it gives light to everyone in the house. In the same way, let your light shine before others, that they may see your good deeds and glorify Your Father in heaven. Matthew 5: 14-15 (NIV).

Reflection of an Abundant Heart

As I approached the city limits of Dallas, I witnessed a sky filled with gray clouds. The sky, eerily similar to the previous day, fascinates me. Okay, God, I get it! This is a message you really don't want me to miss!

Though the clouds obstructed the sun rays, its bright light could not be denied. The reflection broke through, its beams scattered by a stratocumulus barrier. Each shaft of light splitting the lumpy sheet of grey clouds at a different angle or direction. Each ray dispersed and reflected the source of light, directing attention back to its origin. Despite the dense cover, the sun burst through and set the sky ablaze.

We live in a world of difficult circumstances. Facing the business of daily living creates enough stress to cause dark moods.

The evening news often weighs us down.

Daily we learn of friends and family who face monumental situations.

Often, we find ourselves confronting a crisis for which we are unprepared. When the unexpected or tragic occurs, clouds of life threaten our peace.

As I allow the Son to shine through the cloudy circumstances of my life, I reflect His love and presence in my life. Frequently unknown to me, the dispersed rays shine into other's lives, offering the encouragement they need.

The way Christians handle adversity should set us apart from an unbelieving society. The presence of Holy Spirit strengthens us to face trials with grace. Like the rays of sunshine, we point others to the source.

As I listen, Holy Spirit speaks to my heart.

There is light behind the cloud!

Hang on, Child!

Let me show you how I can work through this one!

Prayer of an Abundant Heart

Powerful Father, Loving Shepherd, Sweet Holy Spirit,

Forgive me when I fail to trust You.

You've worked in many situations in my life and carried me through unspeakable crises.

When circumstances threaten my peace and joy, help me give each problem to you.

Make my life the kind of light that reflects Your love and glorifies You.

You alone are the source of my strength, the light and joy of my life.

Personal Reflection

You Cast, He'll Catch

God's Word

Cast all your anxiety on him because he cares for you. (1 Peter 5:7 NIV).

Reflection of an Abundant Heart

Never just a game, baseball emerged as an American cultural phenomenon. It dates to the first official game played in Hoboken, New Jersey in 1846. The sport gained national prominence during the Civil War. When soldiers from different states played to pass time, baseball's popularity spread throughout the nation.

Because of its simplicity and accessibility, anyone, regardless of social class or background could enjoy playing or spectating. More than an athletic contest, baseball evolved with societal changes in the United States. From its inception to the digital age, baseball retained a unique place in American culture. Its deep roots and ability to adapt secured a place as a cultural legacy and connector of generations.

Whether cheering a little leaguer, the high school or college team, or a favorite major league team, true baseball fans immerse themselves in the minutia of the game. They study statistics, collect baseball cards, follow specific players, and critique the details of each play.

Any avid fan recognizes the importance of the catcher. He serves as the team's general. Before the game begins, he puts on all the right equipment to catch whatever is thrown. He handles every ball in the game. He must be ready to adjust to a variety of pitches. Whether a fast ball, curve, slider, sinker, knuckle, splitter, or more, the catcher assumes the position and readies himself to handle any potential throw. He frames the pitch to make it look like a strike.

The catcher protects home plate by standing on the baseline and taking the brunt of the runner attempting to score from third. When the game concludes, he is the dirtiest one on the team. He keeps up with the outs and the pitch count. He views the entire field.

Besides being athletic, the catcher must be mentally and physical tough. He should be observant and accurate with exemplary leadership skills and a bit of fearlessness.

As we observe over time, we understand no one individual exhibits the abilities perfectly every game. Wild pitches get by even the most talented player and sail to the backstop, often allowing the opposing team to score.

Unlike human beings, prone to error, God never misses. He possesses the power and skill to handle anything His children throw at Him. No pitch surprises Him. He sees the entire field and remains alert able to direct the game of life.

The Bible tells us to cast every concern on Him.

Cast your cares on the LORD and he will sustain you; he will never let the righteous be shaken. (Psalm 55:22 NIV).

The dictionary defines cast as to throw something forcefully.

Visualize a game plan. Name the pitches; troubling thought, anxiety, unsolvable situation. Imagine yourself as the pitcher. Hurl the concern with all the strength of a superhero. Because He cares for you, Jesus promises not only to catch your cares but will also carry them.

Contrasted to a baseball catcher, who may not be able to make the play, Jesus never fails to secure anything we entrust to Him. Be assured, He will never throw anything back.

Note: Inspired by my friend, Cynthia Brown. An avid sports fan, especially baseball or anything her children and grandchildren played, she acquired a wealth of knowledge by observation. She shared the original analogy from her personal Bible study with our church congregation and added to my baseball knowledge.

Prayer of an Abundant Heart
Compassionate Lord,
Thank You for the assurance, You care about everything that concerns me.
You tell me to give every care to you. I trust You to carry the burdens of my heart.
I rest confidently in Your power.
I gratefully acknowledge, You are in charge and do not need my help.
I release my burdens to You. Help me resist the urge to pick them up again.

Personal Reflection

_____
_____
_____
_____
_____
_____
_____
_____

Living with Threatening Skies

God's Word

Don't worry about anything; instead, pray about everything. Tell God what you need, and thank Him for all he has done. Then you will experience God's peace, which exceeds anything we can understand. His peace will guard your hearts and minds as you live in Christ Jesus. (Philippians 4:6-7 New Living Translation).

Reflection of an Abundant Heart

An ominous evening sky with accompanying dark, gloomy clouds promised a menacing storm. A damp heaviness hung in the air throughout the entire day. The sky looked as if it would burst at any moment flooding the earth. Strong winds reminded even casual observers – inclement weather threatened. Those who planned outdoor activity investigated safer alternatives. The forecast predicted unsafe conditions, but so far none materialized. Still, an intimidating threat captivated the storm chasers.

Because my Granny Carr experienced West Texas tornadoes, storms terrorized her. I remember as a little girl being packed up and taken to the storm cellar. My apprehension of any storm threat paled in comparison to my fear of the rattlesnakes which often made their home in my grandparent's cellar.

Mawmaw Dooly's home in town lacked the perceived security of a storm cellar. When threatening clouds darkened, she herded her grandchildren under the kitchen table, forced us to huddle, and covered us with pillows. Because my youthful experience never included the damage of a Texas tornado, I failed to understand the urgency fueling my grandmother's distress. This exercise seemed foolish to me, because the storm never came.

Unfortunately, storms sometimes do occur and wreak havoc on unsuspecting and unprepared victims. Our world produces ominous conditions. Sometimes literal storms threaten our physical well-being. Other times emotional or spiritual tempests lurk, causing unresolved anxiety.

An endless list of what ifs cause us to live as if we are preparing for a storm.

What if I am rejected?

What if I get sick?

What if someone in my family gets sick?

What if someone I love dies?

What if I don't have enough money saved for college? For retirement?

What if I have an accident?

What if I lose my job?

What if I can't pay my bills?

Living under the cloud of worry fails to solve any of life's perplexing questions. Rather, the anxiety becomes a paralyzing fear.

Like a storm that never materializes, worry stops our progress and robs us of daily joy.

Anxiety about the future steals the enjoyment of the present.

Winnie the Pooh gets it. "What day is it?" he asks Christopher Robin.

"It's today" Christopher replies.

Winnie the Pooh is excited, "My favorite day. Yesterday, when it was tomorrow, it was too much day for me." (A.A. Milne)

God never intended for us to live in a state of anxiety. Jesus instructed us to live fully in the moment.

Therefore, do not worry about tomorrow, for tomorrow will worry about itself. Each day has enough trouble of its own. (Matthew 6:34 NIV).

We experience sweet freedom when we follow the scripture's instruction, release our worries, and trust God to fill us with His peace.

Prayer of an Abundant Heart

Creator and sustainer of the universe,
You control the world and everything in it.
Acknowledging Your control allows me to rest in Your care.
Help me relinquish my concerns to You; health, finances, relationships, national crises.
You reign over all of it and have the power to handle everything.
I concede You do not need my help to keep the world in motion.
Help me to recognize this fact, daily place all my fears in Your hands, and leave them there.

Personal Reflection

_____

_____

_____

_____

_____

_____

_____

_____

_____

_____

Miracle on the Highway

God's Word
I will lie down and sleep in peace, for you alone, O Lord, make me dwell in safety. (Psalm 4:8 NIV).

Reflection of an Abundant Heart

One afternoon I witnessed a miracle. As I drove along the familiar highway, I mentally listed all the things I needed to accomplish that evening. In a single moment, my senses heightened and my preoccupation with the endless to do list shifted to the events unfolding in the lanes directly in front of me.

A work trailer followed a caravan of tractors and mowers along the shoulder of the road. Without warning, a small sportscar sideswiped the trailer. Airborne, the small vehicle flipped across three lanes of traffic. A third vehicle swerved into a guard rail to avoid the accident.

This unusual accident interrupted the normally routine afternoon commute. Attentive drivers slowed to avoid the chaotic scene ahead. One by one vehicles comprising rush hour traffic pulled to the side of the road. Since all lanes were blocked by the accident, we were not going anywhere. After I called 911 to activate the emergency response system, I exited my parked car to offer emergency assistance.

As I approached the overturned car, the driver crawled out without help and appeared to be minimally injured with only a small cut on his head. He expressed no concern for the other people involved in the accident. The very inebriated young man repeatedly yelled, "Don't call the cops!"

Two open, half consumed containers of alcohol lay in the floor board of the car. Though the other vehicles sustained significant damage, fortunately, no one required treatment for serious injuries.

The shared experience immediately bonded the dozen or so people who stood outside our parked cars on the side of the highway. We realized the miracle we witnessed and gratefully acknowledged an averted tragedy.

The work crew spent the afternoon mowing along the roadway with a trailer slowly following behind. Everyone escaped injury. Grateful for safety, the owner of the business expressed concern for his employees and equipment.

A small SUV sustained significant damage. Its driver swerved, taking out a good portion of the guard rail but avoiding a collision with the flipping vehicle or with oncoming traffic. Shaken but without physical injuries, he waited for emergency assistance. The cars immediately behind the accident scene had recently stopped at a traffic light. Because we traveled at less than the posted speed limit, traffic halted without creating a domino effect.

Definitely not the way you choose to make new friends. We shared our gratitude. Our CPR training would not be utilized today.

Only one person failed to appreciate of the gravity of the situation. The driver who caused the accident seemed oblivious to the gracious miracle which allowed him to go to jail by way of the hospital emergency room, rather than ending up in the morgue.

Leaving work, I never anticipated an encounter with a drunk driver at 5:30 in the afternoon. A matter of seconds spared my direct involvement in the accident.

We live in an imperfect world. One filled with danger. In a heartbeat, life could end, or be irrevocably changed. Insurance will repair the property damage, and life will go on for all of us. Perhaps we will all be a little more cautious and vigilant. Those who recognized what we witnessed as a miracle continue our life journey with much more gratitude.

Prayer of an Abundant Heart

Ever loving Lord,
As I lay my head on my pillow,
I pray with a grateful heart.
Thank You for protection.
I narrowly missed colliding with an out-of-control car.
Just a few seconds made the difference.
I thank You for the quick responsiveness of the SUV driver.
I ask that You bless each of the people I met in a special way.
Give them peace of mind and a sense of Your presence and watch care over them.
I pray especially for the driver who caused the accident.
I pray this event with the resulting penalty causes him to examine his situation and teaches him the lessons he needs to learn.
Help me to live with a new awareness of Your care for me.

Personal Reflection

_____

_____

_____

_____

_____

_____

_____

The Pathway to Royalty

God's Word

The Lord your God is with you, the Mighty Warrior who saves. He will take great delight in you; in his love he will no longer rebuke you, but will rejoice over you with singing. (Zephaniah 3:17 NIV).

Reflection of an Abundant Heart

A shady country road winds through an arching canopy of oak trees, giving the allusion of protection from the elements. The path beckons travelers to continue exploring the grand entrance leading to a new adventure.

Crowns of trees form the uppermost layer of the forest known as the canopy. Crowns and canopies denote royalty. In architecture canopies symbolize a royal presence. In the churches of the Middle Ages the canopy symbolizes divine presence.

Could this road I travel under a canopy of oaks be a royal pathway?

This idea sparks my imagination.

My daily routine resembles nothing regal. In fact, I perceive myself fulfilling the role of a servant much more than royalty.

However, God views me differently. As a father loves his child, He delights in me, loves me, and rejoices over me. He reigns as the Eternal King of heaven and earth, and calls me His daughter.

Doesn't that make me a Princess?

I accept this royal assignment and recognize my

purpose. The path I travel serves as my coronation. This royal status carries no sense of entitlement. Rather my position carries with it an awesome responsibility. I possess an unlimited inheritance, not to be horded but freely shared.

God, my Father, reigns as the King of Kings. I am a member of His royal family. Living with confidence, He commissions me to walk the path of royalty and use my royal resources to make a difference in the lives of those I encounter.

Prayer of an Abundant Heart

Eternal King,
I am in awe that You call me Your child, a cherished daughter. Help me to see myself as You see me.
Though unworthy, I desire to be all You created me to be.
Help me to walk in the confidence and security that Your love provides.
Make me a reflection of that love to everyone I meet.

Personal Reflection

_____

_____

_____

_____

_____

_____

_____

_____

_____

_____

_____

_____

_____

_____

_____

_____

_____

_____

_____

_____

_____

_____

_____

_____

_____

_____

_____

_____

_____

_____

_____

_____

_____

_____

_____

_____

_____

_____

_____

_____

_____

Eagles Are Not the Only Birds That Soar

God's Word

He parted the heavens and came down; dark clouds were under his feet. He mounted the cherubim and flew; he soared on the wings of the wind. (2 Samuel 10-11 NIV).

Reflection of an Abundant Heart

Birds mesmerize me. Territorial hummingbirds live in my back yard and dive bomb each other when one threatens the other's food source. Birds remain plentiful as long as the feeders stay full of seeds.

They come in all shapes, sizes, and colors. Each species displays individual habits with regard to mating, nesting, and caring for their young. Some choose to settle in bird houses, while others construct nests in the trees. Still others seek the protection from predators by building nests in the center of rose bushes surrounded by thorny stems.

Led by instinct, each spring the barn swallows find their way back to the eaves of porches. There they lay eggs and stay protecting the nest until the newly hatched chicks grow strong enough to survive alone.

On occasion Texans observe hawks and more rarely eagles. The beautiful birds circle and soar through the sky putting on a magnificent aerial display.

Traveling Texas highways, drivers frequently encounter turkey vultures, sometimes also called buzzards. These birds feast on the dead carcasses of the latest roadkill.

Considered the scavengers of the road, they rarely kill any animal. Instead, they wait for death to occur from other causes and take advantage of the meal left by unfortunate circumstances. They feed their chicks by regurgitating undigested food from a pouch in their throat called the crop. They protect themselves in much the same way by vomiting on any would be predator.

Though their habits disgust our sensibilities, they serve the ecosystem by disposing of the dead carcasses on the highway or dead animals in the fields. They live and forage in communities but sometimes venture out on their own to scavenger for food. Keen eyesight serves to identify their next meal.

When positioned on the ground, the large bird appears awkward and obnoxious. With great effort, flapping their wings and hopping around, the vulture takes flight. At a distance an observer doesn't notice the disgusting habits or the ungainly appearance. Once in flight he soars as beautifully as any hawk or eagle.

Like the birds, humans display diversity in their habits and purpose. Life's experiences shape our attitudes and prejudices. Sometimes we look at others and judge them ugly or disgusting. We may even view ourselves as unattractive and useless.

Observing habits of the vulture provides perspective.

God made each creature for a unique purpose. Even those disdained by the world's standards display glorious beauty and strength. When we fulfill God's purpose for our lives, like the vultures, we soar just as beautifully as any of His creatures.

Prayer of an Abundant Heart
God, creator of all nature,
Thank you for the lesson of the buzzard.
You do not make mistakes.
You created each of us for a purpose.
Even when I feel less than beautiful, I know that You view me as a
beautiful creation.
You see me for what I can be and encourage me to soar, like the vulture,
the hawk, and yes, even as the eagle soars.
Help me to realize my full potential – to be all that You created me to
be.

Personal Reflection

_____
_____
_____
_____
_____
_____
_____
_____
_____
_____
_____
_____
_____
_____
_____
_____

The Real Thing

God's Word

But seek first his kingdom and his righteousness, and all these things will be given to you as well. (Mathew 6:33 NIV).

Reflection of an Abundant Heart

Low-lying clouds accompanied a blazing sun. Moisture from the clouds created an uncommonly steamy June morning. As I topped the hill leading to the county road out of our neighborhood, I squeezed my eyes tightly and refocused. Something about the familiar landscape appeared very different. A vast lake lay in the distance beyond the field ahead. I observed a large body of quiet, still waters covering the normally green, grass-covered fields.

From the top of the hill an illusion of something beautiful promised cool calm water. In reality, a dense thick fog covered the familiar road and surrounding fields. What appeared to be an oasis hid the possibility of unanticipated danger.

How often the world tempts us to pursue an illusion, accepting the promise of momentary pleasure. The counterfeit frequently offers a really good imitation of the real thing. We expend endless energy and passion looking for the possibility of an unrealistic dream. Even when we achieve the specific goal or fulfill a fantasy, often a feeling of emptiness results.

Unfulfilled, we ask ourselves, "Why did I want this so

desperately? Was the realization of the dream worth the sacrifice it required?"

Sometimes the answer may be "Yes, the treasure justifies the cost."

At other times, the fantasy proves to be so much better than the reality, leaving us to wonder, "Is this all there is?"

When we insist on pursuing illusive fantasies, we limit God's ability to reveal the purpose He has for us. We settle for the counterfeit instead of allowing Him to fill our lives with true joy.

The temporary fades away. The counterfeit perishes with time. Truth lasts, revealing genuine value.

Prayer of an Abundant Heart

My Sovereign Lord,
Thank You for the reminder that what looks good for the moment may be a mirage, masking dangerous pitfalls.
I trust You and want Your best for me.
I surrender my goals and dreams, releasing my grip.
Lead me, Lord.
Help me not to settle for an imitation, or even for mediocre.
Instead, I wait for Your guidance.

Personal Reflection

_____

_____

_____

_____

_____

_____

Changing Skies

God's Word

Jesus Christ is the same yesterday and today and forever. (Hebrews 13:8 NIV).

Reflection of an Abundant Heart

The Friday morning weather forecast predicted no incumbent weather. Yet, dark clouds moved rapidly across the sun and suddenly the scene changed from bright sunshine to threateningly dark and gloomy. I focused on one particular area of the menacing sky which demanded my attention. Views of the exact spot looked completely different in a matter of moments.

Texans fondly quote the popular adage, "If you don't like the weather in Texas, wait a minute."

I continued to ponder the clouds and recalled the scenery from the prior month. An amazingly colorful display of spring flowers covered the fields along the highway. Now freshly mowed meadows of green replaced spent wildflowers.

Each year as seasons progress, the same roadsides appear completely different. If history serves as a predictor, by summer parched grasses replace green meadows, and the winter landscapes offer little vegetation with brown as the dominate color.

Like the skies and the seasons, our lives constantly change. Days rarely look the same. The world embraces rapidly advancing technology and challenges us to keep up. Before marketing releases a new product, research, and development work on a new and improved model.

Just as I feel comfortable with a version of my word processor, my smart phone, smart television, or other electronic devices, the programmers release another update.

Known for his doctrine of the changing universe, the ancient Greek philosopher, Heraclitus, predicted an ever-changing world. Translations of Heraclitus philosophy continue to be quoted. "Nothing is constant but change." or "The only thing permanent is change."

As the seasons flow from spring, to summer, fall, and winter, the seasons of our lives flow from childhood, to youth, adult, and old age. Each season presents unique challenges and joys.

Like Heraclitus, I observe that the world changes. While I agree that change is constant, it is not the permanent foundation on which we rely.

I cling to a more hopeful philosophy. The only thing constant or permanent is God.

When God created the universe, He made it to function perfectly through every possible change of season and of our lives.

When change threatens to destroy my world and causes doubt, I stand firm on this principle. God does not change. He is the solid foundation upon which I can build my life.

Prayer of an Abundant Heart

Holy Trinity:
Father, Son, Holy Spirit
You existed before time and created the universe.
Such knowledge is too wonderful for me to comprehend.
Awestruck, I behold Your creation.
As I consider all the intricacies and design of the human body,
I worship You for I am fearfully and wonderfully made.
Thank You for every amazing thing in creation.
Thank You for trusting us to be the caretakers of all You made.
When questions and doubts arise, help me remember —
You are always present—loving, sustaining and upholding.
You, O Lord, are my rock and my salvation.
I build my life on You.

Personal Reflection

_____

_____

_____

_____

_____

_____

_____

_____

_____

_____

_____

_____

_____

_____

Requirements

God's Word

He has shown you, O mortal, what is good. And what does the Lord require of you? To act justly and to love mercy and to walk humbly with your God. (Micah 6:8 NIV)

Reflection of an Abundant Heart

The fluffy white clouds decorating the bright blue morning sky fail to obscure the brilliant light of the sun. I adjust my sunglasses, pull down the visor, and stretch taller in my seat, trying to block the blinding rays of the sun. I cannot see the speedometer or any of the other gauges on my dash.

Light fills every space of the sky. Ignoring the brilliance is impossible. Diverting my focus from the road is not an option. I might avoid the light by changing directions, but then I would not reach my destination. I need to get where I am going. I must fulfill obligations and meet the expectations others have of me.

The bright light persists and demands my attention. An almost audible voice in my spirit delivers a clear message. "I want first place! I am a jealous God!"

God is crazy about me. He loves me unconditionally and passionately.

In the Old Testament book of Deuteronomy 4:24 (NIV), I read, *For the Lord, your God, is a consuming fire, a jealous God.*

Paul delivers Christ's word to the church. *I am jealous for you with a godly jealousy. (2 Corinthians 11:2 NIV).*

What is the response of my heart to this kind of love?

My heart desires to be all He wants me to be. So, I answer, "Yes, Lord. You have my full attention. What do you require of me?"

I recall Jesus' words.

Love the Lord your God with all your heart and with all your soul and with all your mind. This is the first and greatest commandment. And the second is like it. Love your neighbor as yourself. All the Law and the Prophets hang on these two commandments. (Matthew 22:37-40 NIV).

The crystal-clear reply, "Love me, your God, with all your heart. Love yourself as I love you. Then you will be able to love others as you love yourself."

Prayer of an Abundant Heart
Father God,
Thank You for loving me so passionately and sending your son to show me how to live in this world.
Thank you, Christ, my Savior, for giving Your life for me. I commit my priorities to You.
With Your help, I give You first place in my life.

Personal Reflection

A Higher Way

God's Word

For my thoughts are not your thoughts, neither are your ways my ways, declares the Lord. As the heavens are higher than the earth, so are my ways higher than your ways and my thoughts than your thoughts. (Isaiah 55:8-9 NIV).

Reflection of an Abundant Heart

White, feathery clouds heightened the intensity of a brilliantly colored blue sky. The beautiful July day sharply contrasted with the bleary weather of the previous week I dreaded this unscheduled commute into the city.

Sadness engulfed my spirit and tears flowed easily. Heartbroken, I reflected on the anguish of my friend. Suffering and pain characterized her infant daughter's life. Caring for the special needs of their little girl consumed the family's life for more than a year. The family's grief now replaced their baby girl's physical agony.

Any loving mother would gladly exchange her life for the health and happiness of her child. Unfortunately, willingness to trade places with a hurting child failed to change the situation. I ached for my friend, and identified with the experience of supporting a child during a life-threatening illness. I relived painful memories and struggled to make sense of the questions swirling in my head. Ultimately, my daughter survived, while my friend's daughter did not. Though I identify with some of her pain, I can never fully understand the depth of her distress or the emptiness of her arms.

My spirit questions.

Why?

Why are some babies born less than perfect?

What went wrong with the child's development?

We search for a reason, for anything offering a reasonable explanation. We long to understand.

Why?

Why would an innocent baby have to endure such intense pain and suffering? Why are some children healed, while others are not?

Deafening silence responds to our cries for a reason. Job wrestled with "Why?"

God allowed Job to question, and He is big enough to handle all our doubts.

He invites us to approach Him with confidence.

Let us then approach God's throne of grace with confidence, so that we may receive mercy and find grace to help us in our time of need. (Hebrews 4:16 NIV).

Though my questions remain unanswered, He allows me to ask. His reply assures He is with me, will never forsake me and cares for all my concerns.

He collects each tear in a bottle and understands my pain. The Psalmist reminds us,

You have seen me tossing and turning through the night. You have collected all my tears and preserved them in your bottle! You have recorded everyone in Your book. (Psalm 56:8 TLB).

Scripture describes heaven with promises of no sickness, pain, or death. One day, God will perfect everything flawed by earthly standards. Death freed Molly's little body and made her whole and healed. Those left to grieve, struggle to accept the tragedy and move forward.

As long as we remain on earth, we endure the

consequences of a broken world.

He never promised His children, a life without pain, suffering, loss and ultimately death. We stand in the knowledge that He will carry us through any circumstance we face. In times of greatest distress, I cling to and trust Him to sustain and bring good from all things, especially those I do not understand.

Prayer of an Abundant Heart

Holy Comforter,
Thank You for my friend and her abiding faith and trust in You.
Thank You for her precious infant daughter, whose brief life touched so many.
Help me to remember the lessons she taught us and to treasure the memories of sweet times.
Help me to surround the family with prayers and words of encouragement.
Strengthen my sweet friend and hold her close to You in the days ahead as she continues to grieve with empty arms.
Give each member of the family a sense of Your presence as they seek to find a new normalcy and move forward with a new sense of purpose for their lives.
Help us to recognize that life is precious, to be lived fully and never taken for granted.
Show me what You have for me to do today.

Personal Reflection

_____

_____

_____

_____

_____

Flight of the Butterfly

God's Word

Therefore, if anyone is in Christ, the new creation has come: The old has gone, the new is here! (2 Corinthians 5:17 NIV).

Reflection of an Abundant Heart

It started as an attempt to divert rain water. A small corner of the yard bordered by grass on three sides and the driveway on the fourth. I cleared weeds and grass and created a 3x6 foot garden bed.

A master gardener friend gifted small starter plants resulting from the thinning of her own beds. I moved a few Irises from another area of the yard and positioned Kreg's Blue Mist and Coneflowers throughout the bed. Never very good at follow through where plants are concerned, I pretty much ignored them. I let the sprinkler system give them a periodic drink but otherwise contributed little to their survival. Imagine my surprise when they bloomed and butterflies found them.

Each fall the entire bed dies back and gets mulched. New plants emerge each spring. They aren't the prettiest flowers, looking more like weeds. However, beauty is not their purpose. They exist to feed the butterflies.

So began my obsession with pollinators. I attended classes held by local master gardeners. I researched which flowers and shrubs attract butterflies, bees and birds and do best in our area with minimal care. I learned about Monarch Waystations.

The resulting pocket gardens provide places to feed and water wildlife. The areas also offer areas of quiet respite to nurture my soul.

All summer the butterflies feast on the nectar from colorful flowers. I watch as they busily flit from flower to flower and flutter through the air. Each time I leave my garage, a kaleidoscope of butterflies greets me, and I smile.

Some butterflies live only a few weeks while others overwinter or migrate and may live for months. They develop through the process of metamorphosis; a Greek word meaning transformation or change in shape. Egg, larva, pupa and adult complete the stages of metamorphosis, producing a very different mature form.

Once they emerge from the chrysalis, they work diligently to accomplish their purpose, to pollenate and reproduce. The butterflies' limited lifespan requires persistence to fulfill their reason for existing.

More than the insect itself, I love the symbolism ascribed to these beautiful creatures. They represent transformation, hope, and new beginnings. The emergence of a butterfly pictures a powerful metaphor for individual growth.

Experiencing spiritual rebirth, we embrace change and freedom from old behaviors and limitations leading to possibilities and a new way of life.

The butterfly's essential struggle strengthens its wings. Likewise, challenges of life develop character and inner strength of the individual.

As the caterpillar lets go, the butterfly signifies releasing the past and embracing new potential. It encourages joy and pursuit of goals and dreams.

Butterflies embody joy and grace.

Observing the butterfly reminds us to find beauty in life's small fleeting moments and appreciate the wonder of simply existing.

Never waste time or miss an opportunity.

Accomplish what you can.

Live in the moment.

Enjoy the abundant life God provides.

Prayer of an Abundant Heart

Creator of all nature,

Thank You for the joy I feel as I watch the butterfly take flight.

Remind me to follow their example, living to accomplish my purpose.

Help me not to take these amazing creatures for granted.

I am grateful for the daily opportunities You reveal.

Continue to reveal spiritual truths through nature and Your creation.

Don't let me miss the lessons You want me to learn and to share.

Nature calls me to worship.

I praise You, oh Lord, the Creator of the Universe.

Personal Reflection

Amazing Love

God's Word

For God so loved the world, that he gave his only begotten Son, that whosoever believeth in him should not perish, but have everlasting life. (John3:16 KJV).

Personal Reflection

Anna Barlett Warner traced both maternal and paternal roots to Puritan Pilgrams. Born in 1827, she lived with her parents in New England. Her mother died when Anna and her sister, Susan were young children. Her father, a successful lawyer, lost most of his fortune in the Panic of 1837. The family moved from their New York mansion to a dilapidated Revolutionary War-era farmhouse near West Point, New York. In 1849, to help support their family, the sisters embarked on careers as authors, writing under pen names.

In 1860, Anna wrote a bestselling novel, "Say and Seal" where the words to "Jesus Loves Me" first appeared. In the story, Sunday School teacher, Mr. Linden comforts his student, Johnny Fax. The teacher spoke the words to soothe the dying child.

Neither sister married. Devout Christians, they held regular Bible studies for West Point Cadets. Anna wrote a fresh hymn for her Sunday School class each month. When on military duty, the cadets sang "Jesus Loves Me."

Dwight D. Eisenhower graduated the year of Anna's

death and was believed to be one of the last cadets to attend their classes.

Because of the popularity of the song and their contribution to the spiritual well-being of the soldiers, both sisters were buried with military honors, the only civilians buried in West Point Cemetery. Their home, Good Crag, stands as a National Shrine and a museum in the Warner sister's honor.

Before I fully understood Jesus' love for me, I learned and sang this familiar hymn. These words took root in my soul and served as a touchstone for many difficult circumstances throughout my life. The lyrics assured me, no matter the situation, He loved me and would never abandon me.

Jesus Loves Me

Jesus loves me! This I know,
For the Bible tells me so;
Little ones to Him belong;
They are weak, but He is strong.
Refrain:
Yes, Jesus loves me!
Yes, Jesus loves me!
Yes, Jesus loves me!
The Bible tells me so.

Jesus loves me! This I know,
As He loved so long ago,
Taking children on His knee,
Saying, "Let them come to Me."

Jesus loves me still today,

Walking with me on my way,
Wanting as a friend to give
Light and love to all who live.

Jesus loves me! He who died
Heaven's gate to open wide;
He will wash away my sin,
Let His little child come in.

Jesus loves me! He will stay
Close beside me all the way;
Thou hast bled and died for me,
I will henceforth live for Thee.

Such amazing, sacrificial love demands a response.

The words penned by Anna Warner in the nineteenth century ring true to every generation. This hymn presents the gospel in a way children understand while challenging each believer to respond to a call to live for Him.

Trying to trap Jesus, the Pharisees inquired, *which is the greatest commandment in the Law?" (Matthew 22:36 NIV)*

Jesus referred to the scripture. The Jewish leaders surely got the reference. They recited the Shema at least twice a day. Torah instructed the Israelites,

Hear, O Israel: The Lord our God, the Lord is one. Love the Lord your God with all your heart and with all your soul and with all your strength. These commandments that I give you today are to be on your hearts. Impress them on your children. Talk about them when you sit at home and when you walk along the road, when you lie down and when you get up. (Deuteronomy 6:4-7 NIV)

Jesus didn't stop with loving God. He added loving others. Jesus replied:

Love the Lord your God with all your heart and with all your soul and with all your mind. This is the first and greatest

commandment. And the second is like it: Love your neighbor as yourself. (Matthew 22:37-38 NIV)

Christ clearly mandated a sacrificial kind of love. Accept His gift of love. Come to Him with the faith of a little child. Love God completely – with body, heart. and soul. Reach out and love like Jesus loves.

Note: Information regarding the Warner family and the history of "Jesus Loves Me" was gained from an internet search.[1]

Prayer of an Abundant Heart

Triune God,
With a heart full of gratitude, I bow before You.
Thank You for Salvation through Jesus Christ.
Thank You for a legacy of faith; for parents and grandparents who modeled faith and trust.
Thank You for Sunday School teachers and family who taught me Bible truths and songs of faith.
Thank You for music that leads me to worship.
Because You loved me, I commit to live for You.
Help me see others as You see them and love as Jesus loved.
Break my heart for what breaks Yours. Give me opportunities to share Your amazing love with those I encounter.

Personal Reflection

_____

_____

_____

_____

_____

_____

[1] (ND, 2021)

Glimpses of Holiness,
A Christmas Reflection

God's Word
So is my word that goes out from my mouth: It will not return to me empty, but will accomplish what I desire and achieve the purpose for which I sent it. (Isaiah 55:11 NIV).

Reflection of an Abundant Heart
Music speaks to my soul. I especially love Christmas music —traditional, secular, sacred, contemporary. I love it all. Knowing the history and inspiration often enhances my appreciation of songs. In December 2019, I read an article relating the history of O Holy Night. The short history astounded me, piqued my interest and stimulated a quest to learn more about the author and composer of the Christmas classic.

A parish priest from Roquemaure, France commissioned Placide Chappeau to produce a new work for debut on the church's newly renovated organ on Christmas Eve, 1847. As a child, Chappeau sustained a gunshot wound resulting in the amputation of his hand. Though educated in literature and law and known for his poetry, he earned a living in his father's wine-merchant business. An avowed atheist and anti-cleric, he drifted away from faith and the church. Despite his personal lack of faith, he accepted the commission to write for the Christmas celebration.

In preparation for writing, he carefully read Luke 2

and tried to imagine the thoughts and feelings associated with such an event. Recorded tradition reports Chappeau completed the lyrics on a stagecoach in route to Paris and presented them to Adolphe Charles Adams, a composer of Jewish descent. An abolitionist, Unitarian minister translated the French carol into English prior to the United States Civil War.

Dr. David Jeremiah wrote in Turning Points 2019, "Now don't ask me to explain it all. God works in mysterious ways. I cannot explain how a Christmas Carol written by a nonreligious Frenchman, set to music by a Jewish man who didn't celebrate the Lord's birth, and translated into English by a Unitarian preacher could capture the hearts of us all for the last 172 years. Think of it this way. If the Lord could use those three individuals to spread the message of the Gospel through this carol. He can certainly use you and me."

I wholeheartedly agree with Dr. Jeremiah's conclusion. God can and will use any method necessary to draw people to Himself. However, another thought troubles me.

Though Chappeau learned the scriptures as a child and apparently carefully studied Luke's account of Jesus birth, I found no reference in the history of the hymn (or of either lyricist or composer) of a life-altering encounter with Christ. They knew about Jesus and His mission. However, knowing about Christ isn't enough. Intellectual head knowledge differs drastically from an intimate encounter with God, submitting heart and life and making Him LORD.

If God used these men, who seem far from Him, He can use all of us. Imagine what God could have accomplished if they allowed the truth of the gospel to permeate their hearts and souls.

What do we know that Chappeau did not? It was not a holy night. It was an ordinary night with ordinary people.

Because of Emmanuel—God with us—the night became holy.

Still today, He uses ordinary people like you and me. We may lack the talent to create a masterpiece, but as we follow faithfully, He reveals and gives light. He provides glimpses of His holiness, so we can sing with awe and wonder, "Fall on your knees, O hear the angels voices, O night divine, O Holy Night!"

Prayer of an Abundant Heart

Dear Jesus, Christ of Christmas,
I celebrate the miracle of Your coming to this world.
Emanuel, God with us, You provide all the gifts of advent; hope, peace, joy and love. I am never alone.
Beyond knowledge about You, I seek personal, deepening relationship with You.
The songs of faith become more than words and beautiful music. They testify to the transformation You bring to a life fully devoted to You. My heart sings with conviction and joy.

Personal Reflection

_____

_____

_____

_____

_____

_____

_____

_____

He is Coming Back

God's Word

"Look, he is coming with the clouds," and "every eye will see him, even those who pierced him"; and all peoples on earth "will mourn because of him." So shall it be! Amen. "I am the Alpha and the Omega," says the Lord God, "who is, and who was, and who is to come, the Almighty." (Revelation 1:7-8 NIV).

Reflection of an Abundant Heart

Texas sunsets and sunrises produce awe-inspiring skies.

Each time I witness God's handiwork, I wonder how tomorrow's sky will compete. Yet every day, He does it again. Each evening's sunset appears as spectacular than day before

The sun blazes, and an arch of light covers the sky. Colors of blue, yellow, green red, orange and pink appear.

Occasionally, I observe a rainbow and reflect on God's promises. The rainbow symbolizes His promise to never again destroy the world by flood.

Scripture records many promises upon which we can rely. His assurance to return for His children provides the hope of eternity with God.

Every day, I examine the sky to observe the beauty of creation.

One day, as I search the sky, Christ will break through the clouds!

Everyone will see Him.
We shall behold Him!
Wow!
I cannot imagine a better reason to continue searching the skies.

Prayer of an Abundant Heart

Lord of my life,
I praise You.
I recognize Your rightful place as King of my life.
I honor You with all I am.
I want to be found faithfully serving when You return.
Use me to share your love with those I encounter.
As I continue to search the skies, I eagerly anticipate Your return.
Come, Lord Jesus, Come.

Personal Reflection

_____

_____

_____

_____

_____

_____

_____

_____

_____

_____

_____

_____

References

ND. (2021, June 17). *The Story Behind The Song "Jesus Loves Me".*
Retrieved from Praise Broadcasting Network:
https://www.pbnradio.com/blog/2021/6/17/the-story-behind-
the-song-jesus-loves-me

About the Author

Native Texan, Wanda Strange resides in Bluff Dale, Texas. Wanda's active life prioritizes family and friends. An active member of her church and community, she devotes time to reading, writing, and volunteering. She loves music, books, and passionately pursues time with family and friends. Her passion for people provides motivation to share stories of God's faithfulness. Her published works include *Legacy: Memories, Mysteries, Musings: Emerging from the Crucible: Enduring God's Refining Fire:* and *Abundant Heart; A Five-Year Gratitude Journal.*
wstrange0306@gmail.com
https://www.facebook.com/wandadoolystrange/

www.ingramcontent.com/pod-product-compliance
Lightning Source LLC
Chambersburg PA
CBHW061143040426
42445CB00013B/1526